Navy Writer

Navy Writer

How to Write Navy Evals and Awards

Adams & Stregles

Copyright © 2010 by Military Writer

All Rights Reserved

ISBN 978-0-9843563-2-4

Published and Designed by Military Writer

Printed in the United States of America

Dedicated to the men and women serving our country
around the world, far from home and family

෪ඏ

Introduction

We love the Navy and the opportunities for adventure and advancement it offers but we have to realize that, in an organization as big as the Navy, it's easy to get lost in the shuffle. It's easy to be overlooked and not be recognized as the top notch Sailor that you've become. And because of that, it's up to us, as individuals, to make an effort to make sure we get credit for the work we've performed so that we remain competitive for promotion and the opportunities we've earned. It's very important that we spend the time necessary to produce an accurate and effective annual evaluation.

This book is not about the administrative or official regulations that govern the preparation of Navy evaluations and awards. It doesn't specify timelines or rules of grammar. There are already plenty of books and regulations that address those necessary details. Instead, this book focuses on how to write it, how to say it, and how to get the most out of your achievements.

Please see www.navywriter.com/book/corrections.htm for any corrections that were found after publishing. Comments may be directed to editor@militarywriter.com.

Writing a Navy Eval

It's an unfortunate fact of military life that no matter how hard you work or how many hours you put in, all your efforts will have been wasted if they aren't recorded on a single sheet of paper —your Evaluation. The single most important factor in whether you get promoted is your annual performance evaluation. That single sheet of paper affects your chances for promotion, your assignment options, training opportunities, and your entire future in the military. It is vital that you take the time to find out what you need to do in order to meet and exceed requirements for your rating and then prepare. And you have to start early. It takes from six months to a year to build a favorable impression with your supervisor. Then, it's equally important to make sure those achievements get recorded in your Eval and that it's as well written and as accurate as possible.

The success of your annual evaluation depends on much more than the Comments on Performance block. Your actions and preparation over the previous year are the most critical component because without them, there would be nothing to write about! But this short tutorial is focused on getting the most mileage out of the achievements you have now.

Squeezing an entire year of performance into a mere 16 lines is a challenge but if you break the task down into its basic parts, the job becomes logical, less subjective, and easier.

The Comments on Performance block is normally divided into three sections: the Introduction, the main

Accomplishments section, and the Summary. Each of these areas has its own format and purpose. Note that these "sections" within the Comments on Performance block are not marked or labeled as such. It is up to the writer to provide comments that comply with this informal standard. The requirement to follow this format and address the topics required by each section derives from evolving Navy tradition and methodology rather than published guidance. See the following sections that elaborate on the requirements for the Eval introduction, the main accomplishments area, and the summary.

The Eval Introduction

The purpose and goal of the Navy Eval is to accurately and fully describe performance. This is often accomplished by listing the notable achievements of the person being rated. While listing significant achievements does provide some insight into a person's capabilities, it doesn't provide the whole picture. A list of achievements doesn't give any indication as to the character or personality of the ratee. A Sailor might have a long list of impressive accomplishments but be an unruly subordinate with a bad attitude. He or she might be an expert in their field but the absolute worst at sharing experience or getting along with others. And those social qualities are very important, fully as important as a person's technical skills.

So, in addition to describing a person's professional and technical skills, we need a way to convey to the Evaluation's reader his social skills, his integrity, his character, his loyalty and other qualities which aren't apparent when merely reading a list of accomplishments. The introduction is where this is done. Incidentally, these are the only lines where descriptive, subjective terms and adjectives are tolerated and even encouraged.

The definition of subjective is: unsupported or unproven. For example, my opinion of a Sailor may be that he is loyal and leadership material. If I don't provide examples of achievements that demonstrate those qualities, then my statements were merely my own opinion, biased, unsupported by facts, and subjective. The opposite of subjective is objective. Objective statements are statements that are clearly true because they're supported by facts. If I said that YN2 Smith processed 200 Evals, more than any other member of his department, that would be an objective statement because it's demonstrated by facts. If I said YN2 Smith was the most patriotic member of the Navy, that would be a subjective statement because, first, patriotism is difficult to measure, but also because no one knows exactly how patriotic the rest of the Navy is. This statement would be just my opinion and subjective. The introduction of the Evaluation and the summary are the only areas where subjective statements are allowed.

The Eval's Comments on Performance block has 16 lines. Normally, the first two or three lines are used to describe the ratee's character. The area used to introduce the ratee compared to the rest of the block looks like this:

1. Introduction: two or three lines for the rater to describe aspects of
2. character not readily apparent from achievements
3. accomplishment
4. accomplishment
5. accomplishment
6. accomplishment
7. accomplishment
8. accomplishment
9. accomplishment
10. accomplishment
11. accomplishment
12. accomplishment
13. accomplishment
14. accomplishment
15. last accomplishment or first line of summary
16. Summary: one or two lines for the rater to summarize the ratee's performance and make a promotion statement.

Note that there are 16 lines in the Comments on Performance block and a two-line introduction will use up 1/8th of that space. So, while the Introduction is vital and necessary, it should be limited to two lines if possible to allow maximum room for listing achievements.

Introduction Statement Examples:

A superior Sailor with a can-do attitude—always willing to take on more challenging tasks with greater responsibility. Earnest, loyal, and reliable, promote to Petty Officer ahead of peers!

An outstanding and welcome addition to our shop. In just 3 months he has made a huge impact on the unit's efficiency and morale. Not ranked higher solely due to time onboard. Ready for advancement!

Seaman Apprentice Smith is an outstanding and skilled Yeoman. Consistently superior performer. Totally dedicated to mission accomplishment. Intelligent, charismatic team player with natural ability.

Note that these introduction statements are not necessarily the best examples. They are listed to demonstrate the format of the two-line introduction. See the chapter titled, Opening Comment Examples for more examples.

How should you describe the ratee's performance? Think about what this person means to you. Think about how his or her presence has affected your workcenter. What was it like before he or she arrived? How have things improved? What facets of his or her personality stand out the most clearly? When you have it, define that quality in a couple of well-chosen adjectives and then summarize the positive results of that quality.

Below are examples of positive adjectives that might be used to describe your troop. Be careful not to use two different words that describe the same trait. For example if you wrote that a person was, "the epitome of efficiency and effectiveness", those words mean roughly the same thing.

You could have used another word that more expansively described the person's character such as "dependable and efficient".

ambitious	best	competent
active	beneficial	conscientious
adept	bold	cooperative
aggressive	brilliant	confident
adaptable	bright	decisive
astute	capable	determined
admirable	consistent	diplomatic
assured	critical	dynamic
able	conservative	dedicated
agile	commanding	diligent
alert	committed	enthusiastic
accomplished	considerate	energetic
bolstered	creative	efficient

See the chapter titled Positive Adjectives for more examples.

Stratification

Many units insist on stratification statements on the first line of the Eval. Stratification is a word meaning to describe a person's performance compared to their peers. Management wants us to document exactly how the ratee compares to his or her co-workers of equal rank in the workcenter. This means that someone in the work center will be listed as number 1, someone will be ranked as number 2, someone will be judged to be number 3 and so on. This can be a really challenging task as everyone has different skills and excels at one thing or another. We're all good at something. But, if required, it has to be done no matter how hard it is. When ranking your personnel, the following traits should be considered:

- timeliness - shows up to work on time

- dependability - complete assigned tasks without supervision

- appearance - uniform satisfactory and meets fitness standards

- behavior – maturity, respect for authority and off-duty performance

- ability - capable of completing assigned tasks/progressing

A common method of stratifying work center members is to concentrate on one person at a time and rate them 1 to 5 on each of the above categories. Then, add up the scores. The highest score will be number one. The second highest will be number two and so on. Ordering subordinates this way helps to make the process objective and fair.

Stratification Examples:

#1 of 4 Petty Officers--a real go-getter responsible for returning enthusiasm and efficiency to this workcenter!

My #1 of 6 Seaman Apprentices; chosen to represent unit as Sailor of the Quarter, 7th Fleet

#1 of 5 POs! Outstanding leader and top performer who delivered stellar results during Global War on Terrorism

See the section on stratification for more ways to describe a person's performance in relation to their peers.

Format

The format for the introduction (and also the summary) is different than the bullet statement format required in the main body of the Comments on Performance block. The main body of the Comments on Performance block should consist of concrete bullet statements that describe exactly what was accomplished. There is no room for flowery adjectives there. We only want the facts. But, in the introduction, subjective terms and adjectives are tolerated and even encouraged in order to fully describe the ratee's character.

The introduction requires a narrative format although it's OK to use phrases and incomplete sentences. It's OK to capitalize entire words and even phrases but capitalization should be used sparingly. Reserve its use for when you truly need to emphasize something. It's OK to capitalize part of the introduction, as in, "MY BEST WATCH OFFICER EVER! PROMOTE NOW!" but you should only do it for your best troops.

In summary, the Introduction is arguably the most important section of the Eval. It's the portion of the Comments on Performance block that is read first and provides the tone for the entire performance report. It carries the fully qualified opinion of the supervisor. By leaving out a promotion statement here, the rater is saying that, even though I describe this person in glowing terms, I really don't think he should be put in charge of other people. After the Supervisor has documented his or her assessment of the individual's character, he can go on to support that assessment by listing the subject's accomplishments.

Eval Accomplishments

As stated before, the goal of the Eval is to accurately and fully describe performance. While the Introduction provides information on the subject's personality and character, most of the Comments on Performance block is reserved for recording the subjects accomplishments during the reporting period. A list of accomplishments provide a factual window onto a person's abilities, skills, and productivity. The ratio of the number of lines devoted to accomplishments to the number of lines set aside for the introduction give you an idea of the importance the Navy places on technical skill and ability. Technical and professional qualities are critically important to achieving the Navy's mission and, for advancement, fully as important as a person's social and leadership skills. The quickest and most effective way to come up with material for your Eval is to brainstorm first. List all the ratee's accomplishments on a separate sheet of paper. Write down everything that might qualify as a bullet. Nothing is too small or off-limits. Make sure off-duty education, duty qualification, community involvement, and training is addressed too.

One thing that's important to note and that might help you get over your writer's block is that when you're putting together a list of accomplishments, don't hold back! If you're new to Navy Evaluations, you might be reluctant to claim credit for any achievements that you weren't 100% responsible for. You shouldn't be. Most workcenter accomplishments require the efforts of many people working as a team across multiple shifts. If you had any part in one of your department's accomplishments, you're allowed to claim it and list it on your Eval. A supervisor will often list the same achievements, over and over, to beef up several people's Evals so don't hesitate to claim those accomplishments as your own. As a rule of thumb, if you had any part in a project, from documenting it in a log to turning a wrench, you can claim it. So claim everything and let your supervisor sort it out.

Comments on Performance Block Format

1. Introduction: two or three lines for describing character
2. Introduction: describe aspects not apparent from accomplishments
3. continued Introduction or first duty-related accomplishment
4. duty-related accomplishment
5. duty-related accomplishment
6. duty-related accomplishment
7. duty-related accomplishment
8. duty-related accomplishment
9. accomplishment
10. accomplishment
11 .accomplishment
12. accomplishment
13. accomplishment
14. accomplishment
15. continuation of last accomplishment or first line of Summary
16 Summary: one or two lines for the rater to summarize the ratee's performance and make a promotion statement.

List Achievements in Logical and Descending Order

After you've brainstormed and came up with a list of accomplishments, sort them into four categories:

duty-related, primary or collateral duties

leadership/mentoring/climate

qualification, training, self-improvement

community service

The reason for sorting the accomplishments into groups is because they are required to be listed in the Eval in a certain order. The list above is ordered by the level of importance. When listing achievements in the Comments on Performance block, the duty-related accomplishments should be listed at the top, on the first line of achievements, right below the Introduction. After listing all the duty-related bullets, then list the other categories in the order shown above. Add your leadership-type bullets, then training and self-improvement bullets and finally community service entries. Keep categories together for ease of reading. Keep in mind that the Navy wants well-rounded people. Your Eval should reflect this; make sure you include bullet statements that represent all the categories shown above and whatever trait the Navy is emphasizing at the moment.

Note that some types of achievements must be listed in Block 44:

- Qualifications Attained During the Reporting Period

- Courses Completed During the Reporting Period

- Civic Activities Beneficial To the Navy

- Awards and Commendations

A suggested number of lines to devote to each topic is:

- Introduction : 2 Lines

- Duty-related : 6 Lines

- Leadership /current hot topic : 3 Lines

- Qualification, training: 2 Lines

- Community service : 1 Lines

- Summary : 2 Lines

The duty-related bullets are considered to be the most significant and that's why they're listed first. It is said that reviewers are often in a hurry and can't afford to spend a lot of time reading individual performance reports. They may only glance at the first few lines. So, knowing that we must grab the reviewer's attention in the first few lines, the best accomplishments or bullet statements should be listed first —at the top. The next important accomplishment would be listed second and so on until you reach the "contributed to the Combined Federal Campaign" bullet at the bottom. Personally I think this belief about senior personnel having so little time to review personnel records is an urban legend. Any organization that placed so little importance on the selection process that they spent only a few seconds reviewing records in order to fill their most critical positions would quickly collapse under the weight of its own inefficiency. In my opinion, the reason for listing the bullets in this order is to enhance readability.

Bullet Statement Format

In order to describe accomplishments as directly as possible, without a lot of unnecessary embellishment, the Navy requires them to be written in "bullet statement format". Bullet statement format is the use of phrases and key words to express something and doesn't follow the normal rules of grammar or sentence structure. Examples of bullet statements are:

- Prepared two detachments for deployment

- Reserved space on two freighters

- Rescued seven lost Air Force pilots

The object is to get your point across with as few words as possible.

When it comes to the Navy eval, the bullet statements used should have two parts, the accomplishment and its impact. Each bullet statement should begin with a verb (such as repaired, revived, restored, rescued, etc) and be followed by the impact or positive result of that action.
Note that, in most cases, bullet statements will not be complete sentences. There is very little space in the eval's Comments on Performance block and using this abbreviated method of writing allows the writer to enter as much information as possible while getting right to the point.

Bullets statement structure:

Part 1. Identify the accomplishment.

Part 2. *Describe the accomplishment's positive effect.*

Examples:

- Painted over 3,000 square feet of exterior hull 30 days ahead of schedule; *reduced corrosion by 50%*

- Delivered over 75K gallons of fuel in support of five temporarily assigned minesweepers; *agile ability ensured zero delays to mission*

- Mastered all facets of 7th Fleet's largest distribution element in record time. *Reduced workload on team and raised work center production 30%*

- Supervised emergency repair of air conditioning at Naval Network and Telecommunications Site and *preserved $1.5M of critical equipment*

Make Bullet Statements as Specific as Possible

Be as specific as possible. The overall goal of the performance report is to, as accurately as possible, describe a person's performance. To that end, every statement should be qualified. Every claim should be supported by a quantity and its impact explained. For example, consider the bullet statement:

- Maintained 100% accountability of equipment

To make this bullet more specific, the type of equipment should be listed. And if there were any other factors that made this feat stand out, those should be listed too. When we dig a little deeper, we find more information:

- Maintained 100% accountability of critical medical equipment assigned to 12 units deployed across 300 miles of Southern Afghanistan's most dangerous provinces

Make sure you explain every significant detail of the effort you made to ensure you get credit. For every bullet, run through the Who, What, When, Why, and Where drill. If you give it enough thought you can always make the statement better:

- Assumed responsibility for mismanaged and discrepancy-ridden inventory and, through numerous trips to II MEF outposts spanning 300 miles of Southern Afghanistan's most dangerous provinces, regained positive control of $100,000 worth of critical medical supplies.

Make the Eval as Easy to Read As Possible

Write the bullet statement so that anyone can understand it. Use ordinary day-to-day English and avoid technical jargon unique to your rating. The Evaluation will be reviewed at boards consisting of Senior NCOs from a variety of career fields so it must be understandable to a broad audience and not only someone from your unit or background.

After you've entered all the accomplishments that you can squeeze into the available space, go back and edit them for readability. If possible, make them easier to read. Make sure the bullets are listed in a logical order. Make each bullet statement either one or two or three lines long as appropriate. In other words, try not to end one bullet statement in the middle of a line and start another one on the same line.

Ranked #1 of 5 in Operations department and #4 of 10 assigned. Dependable and capable, an absolute must select for Petty Officer.
- Fearless service as Watch Officer, an E-6 duty! Led a team of joint military personnel providing unparalleled C2 support to the deployed Warfighter
- LEADERSHIP. Set the example for peers and subordinates alike. He is the cornerstone of our team, reduced backlog of reports by 50%, first time in years!
- 100% scrutiny of all message traffic kept center apprised of rapid changes, ahead of fleet. Proven ability to oversee CIC in support of allied operations
- LOYALTY. Assisted in the first-ever CPO induction onboard USS Florida like the USS CONSTITUTION ceremony; instilled core values in new selectees
- Attended Norfolk employment event and processed hundreds of lead cards for potential recruits and forwarded to appropriate Navy Recruiting Stations
- Completed 9 hours toward Engineering degree; poised for greater challenges
- Community-minded. Raised $6,000 for new furniture and renovated school
PN1 Smith is ready for immediate promotion to Chief. He has the experience and motivation to assume more responsibility, strongly recommended for Chief.

In general, the more bullets listed, the better. Six hard-hitting two-line bullets are better than four three-line bullets because they indicate more productivity and action. However don't sacrifice quality for quantity.

In the event that you don't have enough achievements to completely fill the Comments on Performance block, you can expand the Introduction and Summary to three lines each which will reduce the number of lines for accomplishments to ten. The Eval will still look good.

After writing a suitable Introduction and providing an appropriate list of achievements, all that's left to do is provide closing comments.

The Eval Summary

Just as the introduction was a masterpiece of concise expression, the summary must sum up the impression that the writer is trying to convey about the person being evaluated. Normally, one to three lines are used at the bottom of the Comments on Performance block to summarize the tone of the report and provide a promotion statement. It shouldn't take more than two lines to express approval and if three are used, it makes it appear as if the subject of the eval doesn't have many accomplishments.

Sample summary statements:

Exceptional performer. Further challenge with most difficult tasks; promote ahead of peers!

ITC1 Smith has shown tremendous growth, has overcome all obstacles, and is ready for a more challenging billet. A clear choice for Chief Petty Officer, Promote NOW!

Dynamic and distinguished NCO; leads by example; sets high, attainable standards **promote immediately**

Maintained a $10M property account with a 99% accuracy. Best accountability of ten sections. Prime candidate for increased responsibilities. Must Promote!

Driven Petty Officer with outstanding results. Continue to entrust with increasing responsibility--Promote now!

As you can see, the summary isn't an accomplishment. It's a statement much like the introduction that describes how the supervisor views the ratee. And the promotion statement is more or less a requirement. If a promotion statement isn't included in the Summary, it indicates that the rater doesn't think the person should be promoted and is communicating that fact to any future reviewer.

Sometimes, when we get mired in the details of writing an evaluation, we lose track of our goals and despite our best efforts, produce a substandard eval. To get us back on track and remind us of our goals, let's run through the final checklist.

Note: The eval may be written in either 10 or 12 point font. Some people recommend using 12 point with the justification being that it is easier to read and that because of that, reviewers will give it more attention. There is some disagreement about this belief. Using 12 point font is considered by some to be a sign that you don't have enough material and resorted to a larger font to take up space.

Final Checklist

1. Focus on the primary duty. No amount of collateral or additional duties can make up for failure at a Sailor's primary duty. However, collateral duties will help to round out a Sailor's overall performance.

2. Emphasize progression and potential for more responsibility. The eval must show that you were assigned to and excelled at a position that was more advanced than the position held during the previous reporting period.

3. Tell the eval's reader what you accomplished. List your achievements in easy to read bullet statement format. Don't rely on the reader to dig your information out of tangled sentences. Make it obvious!

4. Make the eval easy to read. If possible, confine each achievement to exactly one or two lines. Don't begin a new topic on the same line that another topic ends.

5. Make sure every bullet statement has a positive result or effect listed. Write what the Sailor did and then what the positive outcome was. If appropriate, describe how the accomplishment supported unit goals.

6. Don't use words that only someone from your rating can understand. The eval will be read by Senior NCOs from a variety of career fields and if they can't understand the significance of your work, your records won't be competitive.

7. A good eval should have a recommendation made for a position of more responsibility and experience than is currently held in the closing statement.

Phrases

One of the fundamental steps to good writing is to relax. Although writing the eval is one of the most significant duties you'll encounter during your Navy career, if you start early you'll have plenty of time to revise, correct, and improve your work. The important thing is to just get started without being overly critical of your writing. Once you begin, the rest will fall into place. Below are some phrases to help get the ball rolling.

- a vital member of...managed over 500 reservations and provided over 2,000 bed nights which generated $155,000 in lodging income and...

- accepted a three month interim Superintendent position to provide shop supervision while a new supervisor was being selected

- accounted for over 155 sorties, and 55 thousand gallons of fuel offloaded to a variety of receiving aircraft

- accurately and meticulously processed 555 mission capable receipts contributing to the 1,500 sorties flown

- acquired a multi-base certification that helped alleviate manning shortage at Norfolk NAS

- actions enabled delivery of essential...supplies to awaiting forces in...

- actions led to the unit being lauded by COMPACFLT IG as "best on base"

- adapted to shifting support channels while delivering on time...

- administered over...and assured their wartime worldwide readiness...

- aided in the mission success of the...

- airlifted more than 50 million pounds of cargo and 50 thousand passengers in support of...

- amassed 550 combat hours flying reconnaissance missions in multiple theaters

- an integral factor in the Division earning the coveted COMPACFLT Safety Trophy

- an invaluable team player in...

- an OIF workhorse, he personally issued 1.5M gallons of fuel to over 100 ships on multiple piers

- as a result of dedication to his patients, Balad hospital maintained a 95% survival rate

- assisted in ensuring all team members were cross-trained and capable of all tasks within their crew vehicle

- assisted the efforts to deploy and maintain the...

- assumed the vacant Security Office NCOIC position for a period of ten months and balanced daily duties with increased force protection requirements

- assumed/accepted 50% of military pay workload processing 5,000 transactions with 95% accuracy

- assured 100% unit competency and compliance with...

- assured operational readiness of over 50...

- astute leadership ensured contractor complied with all...

- astute leadership was vital to the Sealift Command moving over 550,000 square feet of cargo

- attention to detail ensured that all sorties launched with 100% on-time take-offs

- attention to detail impressively controlled accuracy and maintained 100% accountability of...

- attention to detail while reviewing travel vouchers evident in the 100% travel regulation compliance and 95% accuracy rate

- battled blistering sand storms in excess of 50 miles per hour, worked around the clock to provide safe passage for...

- certified the safety of over 5.5 million square miles of sovereign airspace

- clearly exceeded the command standard of 95% accuracy

- commitment to quality service allowed section to achieve a 5.5 average customer rating, exceeded NETC 4.0 average

- commitment to service vital to...

- commitment to support unparalleled

- completed all scheduled maintenance actions ahead of schedule while ensuring critical communications remained...

- completed more than 500 scheduled work orders with 95% on-time completion rate

- concurrently, as Division Resource Advisor, managed the unit's annual budget to...

- conducted over 150 dismounted patrols providing a secure path for...

- conducted research on over 500 new item requests using the...

- considering the sheer volume of the task before him...

- consistently demonstrated exceptional professional skills by...

- consistently demonstrated first-class service and superb technical knowledge that...

- consistently demonstrated outstanding professional skills and initiative by assisting with...

- consistently demonstrated professional skill, decisive leadership, and initiative

- continual logistically focused efforts returned all cargo and personnel from Joint Base Iraq to home stations

- continued his dedication to the unit by...

- continued his inspection prowess by...

- contributed immeasurably to...by decoding and processing messages which provided higher headquarter Commanders with vital information on a real-time basis

- contributed significantly to the safety and security of...ensuring...

- contributed to the effectiveness and success of his radio direction finding team in resolving critical radio frequency interference issues in...

- contributed to the effectiveness and success of the Bainbridge by maintaining above-average standards for...

- contributed to the success of...

- contributions were essential to supplying US ground forces with the resources needed to conduct...

- coordinated the movement of 550 tons of equipment and supplies in direct support of OEF

- coordinated with Federal Aviation Administration and local airfields to facilitate...

- coordination, training, and briefings with FSB operators and medical personnel resulted on zero losses or injuries for deployed personnel

- countless contributions at home and abroad positively impacted all involved

- critical attention to detail ensured the rapid movement and repatriation of...

- dedicated over 1500 hours to operations on the...task force, aiding in the detection and eradication of...

- dedication and enthusiasm exhibited by Petty Officer Smith were key to the success of the...

- defended a 10 mile perimeter and guarded three billion dollars in assets which deterred enemy attacks and safeguarded...

- delivered a staggering 99.9% uninterrupted power, the foundation of all fleet air power

- delivered over...while sustaining an impressive 95% maintenance departure rate

- demonstrated exemplary skill, professionalism, and untiring determination in support of the mission

- demonstrated expert knowledge, professionalism, and skill in providing over...under austere conditions

- demonstrated superior performance by key logistical knowledge in support of...

- demonstrated unparalleled leadership supervising 6 tri-service personnel in support of...

- despite constant threat of rocket and mortar attack, leadership of the site's...shop contributed significantly to the success of...

- determination in adhering to NSA policies aided in the Group's "Outstanding" rating during the semi-annual COMSEC Inspection

- devoted to customer support, he provided the link in reaching out to...

- diligence in tracking Close Air Support mission requests guaranteed...

- directed 10 civilians on 300 jobs with a 95% on-time completion rate, smashed NAVEUR 90% goal

- directly contributed to 155 enemy targets being successfully destroyed

- directly responsible for processing of over...recognized by...for...

- directly responsible for the high level of division readiness

- directly supported 50 OEF/OIF units while dispatching $70 million in medical materiel directly to...

- directly supported the squadron's 555 accident-free flying hours

- directly sustained the operations for the Navy's efforts in...

- displayed great dedication to...

- distinguished himself by superior information control of over 10,000 missions, 55,000 tons of cargo and...

- during her tenure with the division, the section training did not experience any failures

- duties performed for the unit in the absence of a unit clerk are so well executed that...

- effectively directed force protection efforts in support of COMSIXTHFLT operations, ensuring the safety of over 1,000 deployed military personnel

- effectively ensured crew protection downrange by...

- efforts and dedication to duty were essential to the success of the Fleet's...mission

- efforts helped ensure that the...continues to be the nation's premiere training academy

- efforts produced the squadron's ability to provide highly qualified, deployment-ready personnel for...

- efforts proved invaluable to the development and operational readiness of...

- efforts smashed NAVEUR goal of 90%

- efforts were instrumental in the success of this high visibility mission

- elevated issues that affected morale and resolved...

- enabled delivery of essential medical supplies to awaiting medics in Baghdad

- enabled on-time medications for over 5,000 customers

- enabled the successful transfer of the critical...mission to...

- enabled the fleet to meet its strategic planning objective as a full spectrum force, both at home and abroad

- encouraged communications and enhanced...

- energetically supported over 55 Aeromedical evacuation missions and helped maintain Staging Facility assets worth...

- enhanced knowledge of COMSEC requirements and fill devices was essential in the execution of over...

- ensured all personnel assigned received mandatory training

- ensured flight safety for 50 sorties per day ISO...

- ensured members' ability to carry on their deployed mission without pay distractions

- ensured more than 50,000 travel vouchers were precisely obligated or updated

- ensured preservation of 155 vital ISR assets through his meticulous coordination with...

- ensured zero product and patient mishaps

- essential to unit's mission success

- established and maintained accurate and available information for reference at all levels of leadership

- established, held a high level of unit readiness

- exceeded all expectations by providing...

- exceeded NAVEUR goal by...

- excellent comprehension and strict enforcement of standards ensured 100% student compliance and...

- exceptional maintenance practices were evident by the continued...

- exceptional oversight of twenty individual file plans was instrumental in the Group's successful...

- exceptional professionalism and initiative have earned the respect of all those around her

- executed 15,000 work orders on time/on target

- executed duties as...flawlessly, maintaining impenetrable/strict entry control into the Weapon Storage Area

- exemplary leadership proved vital to the successful...

- exemplified dynamic management by leading a ten member team to...

- exemplified the highest standards of commitment to...

- exhibited extraordinary service while serving as...

- expert organizational and communication skills, professionalism, and ability to adapt proved invaluable throughout...

- expertly advised USJFCOM...on policies, programs, and procedures

- expertly directed maintenance actions for 1000+ equipment outages directly supporting the...

- expertly maintained the computer network that provided over 1800 hours of continuous service to...

- expertly managed contract compliance which maintained a 96% in-commission rate resulting in...

- extensive job knowledge vital to the successful launch and recovery of over 100 combat sorties

- facilitated 155 medical evacuations, most with major injuries, and aided three aerial deliveries of aid directly to...

- flew over 50 hours in support of...and provided relief to the devastated country of...

- forged a strong partnership with...to maintain rates despite...

- generated 10B in revenue for the Military Sealift Command Working Capital Fund

- guaranteed mission continuity

- guaranteed mission readiness by...

- guaranteed the success of the newly formed squadron as it prepared to fulfill its force protection and air base defense role

- guarded the security of over...

- guided 50 convoys over 1.5 million miles under the most austere conditions to...

- her direct leadership produced five fleet-level award winners and validated her selection as SCPO

- her expeditious assessment under urgent time constraints guaranteed zero delays in the delivery of supplies to war fighters in...

- her methodical warehouse expertise helped validate, inventory, identify and correct over $5.5 million worth of reparable asset overages not accounted for...

- her professional expertise has ensured a year and a half of flawless customer service and...

- her team exceeded Navy Personnel Command's goal of 95% when 99% of all members were paid within five days

- his attention to detail ensured that all pilots were prepared and properly equipped to respond to any threat as well as...

- his brilliant leadership across two directorates directly contributed to the unit's...

- his commendable actions were imperative to mission success

- his comprehensive operational expertise was successfully leveraged by COMSECONDFLT to...

- his dedication to mission accomplishment and personal drive for excellence greatly contributed to...

- his dedication to mission safety and his fellow shipmate's safety earned an unwavering trust and loyalty from his peers and NCOs

- his determination to be the best...and determination toward self development sets the example for all...

- his efforts were paramount in maintaining monthly accountability of weapons and ammunition of NATO nations and contractors

- his exemplary food preparation skills aided Food Service and contributed to...

- his expedient actions prevented potential failures and guaranteed full compliance with...

- his expert knowledge of key duties and responsibilities was vital to mission success and deployment integrity throughout...

- his expertise in this area filled in the gaps in our experience and was vital to...

- his initiative, commitment, and dedication to duty directly contributed to the success and achievements of the...

- his leadership fostered excellence and led to the on time delivery of...with zero findings

- his maintenance proficiency and leadership ability directly contributed to 550 combat sorties and 15,000 bombs delivered!

- his management in relocating and organizing 500 bench stock filters ensured...

- his meticulous attention to detail and comprehensive technical skill was a driving force in the successful...

- his performance, under difficult circumstances, sustained and reestablished operations in...

- his precise expertise guaranteed the safe operation of...that directly supported combat missions for...

- his superb management skills ensured...

- his supervision supported a variety of missions including...

- his talent and dedication to duty led to an efficient delivery and smooth transition into deployment operations

- his technical expertise aided immeasurably in the Bainbridge's stellar performance during Operation Enduring Freedom.

- his technical savvy ensured the Fleet's success

- his tenacious drive was instrumental in the department meeting its goals despite...

- his tireless efforts provided for the successful completion of the...

- his unflagging efforts were directly responsible for a 50% increase in on-time launch rates during the most critical manning shortages experienced in years

- identified and reorganized...and greatly improved equipment accountability and aided in the movement of 1.5K missions

- impacted contingency operations by...

- implemented and applied policies and procedures for efficient and safe use of unit vehicles

- in addition to his demanding staff duties, he completed over 25 hours of community service and...

- in addition to his primary division duties, he spearheaded the department's...

- in this role, he personally ensured the successful upgrade training of personnel located throughout the...

- instructed 155 Army and Air Force war fighters resulting in...

- instructed and evaluated 90 students, cementing a 100% pass rate

- instructed over 300 hours, prepared 500 multi-service warriors in support of overseas contingency operations

- instrumental in monitoring Global Readiness Spares Packages valued at...

- instrumental in successful $1.5 billion UK/US joint procurement which provided...

- instrumental in the expedient recovery of...

- instrumental in the successful execution of 550 operations and the prosecution of 150 high value targets

- kept production at capacity despite 50% deployment

- kept the...rate to less than 1%

- key member of the 2009 EOD Mobile Unit Eight team which captured an impressive 5 trophies and seized Top Honors in Tech Competition

- key to effective management and smooth operation of the...

- key to the admission, stabilization, and survival of over 150 wartime casualties

- knowledge and speedy repair of the...was vital in the...

- launched our 10,000th mission, a historical milestone

- led 155 military and DOD Civilians in the support of two Divisions supporting 3,000 students annually

- led a 55 member installation team in Afghanistan that participated in the construction of 1,500 circuits in ten C2 centers

- led a mobile news team through four theaters of operation highlighting US regional efforts

- led movement of 555,000 lbs of cargo in direct support of OPERATION UNIFIED RESPONSE

- logged over 500 combat hours disseminating time-critical data for battlefield commanders in...

- made major contributions to the effectiveness and success of the unit's Substance Abuse program by...

- made sure all manifests were completed along with routes planned prior to mission

- made sure...systems were 100% capable of...

- maintained 100% accountability of unit personnel and assets during exercise and contingency operations

- maintained a 97% fill rate crushing the Navy standard of 85%

- maintained a constant combat-ready posture

- maintained quality control of 9 major contracts totaling over $5M to provide personnel from 12 nations with power, maintenance, and lodging

- maintained status despite towering obstacles and the loss of...garnered widespread recognition

- maintaining an outstanding 99% accuracy rate

- maintenance actions generated a 95% ready rate

- managed 15 critical base-wide construction projects, delivering over $15 million in base infrastructure improvements

- managed a $5.2 million multi-service supply account with zero errors

- managed a diverse group of over 1,150 military, civilian, and contractor personnel to...

- managed daily schedules for 15 health providers which generated over 15,000 procedures and...

- managed the acceptance inspection of five theater deployable communication packages and ensured the integrity of...$150M in assets

- managed the Plans & Intel section with little or no supervision

- managed the Support Group Government vehicle fleet
supporting over 500 personnel in day to day operations
spanning 55 remote locations

- masterfully pulled 1,555 priority requests, enabling
coalition forces to drop over 55,000 pounds of munitions on
enemy insurgents to protect...

- masterminded the control and security of 55 classified
items garnering a 100% inventory of $5.5 million in assets
with zero security violations

- member of the Vehicle Maintenance team with an in-
commission rate consistently better than the Navy standard
of 90%

- mentored and advised members of the Sudan People's
Liberation Army while simultaneously providing
administration support for...

- meticulous care and knowledge aided in maintaining 100%
accountability of 500 classified assets valued at...

- meticulously managed the processing and out-processing of
2,500 military and civilian personnel

- on his watch, the division successfully mobilized and
deployed 150 Sailors in support of Operations...

- orchestrated processing and airlift requirements for 155
short tons of cargo and 155 deploying members

- outstanding abilities greatly contributed to the squadron
producing 5,500 sorties and 55,500 flying hours in fiscal
year 2010

- outstanding contribution and selfless service were integral to...

- outstanding integrity and devotion to duty were significant factors in...

- outstanding leadership and commitment to excellence were instrumental to the ship's success in...

- outstanding leadership and devotion to duty were instrumental factors in...

- outstanding performance

- over 3,000 arrivals/departures of...on same ramp without incident

- oversaw 555 maintenance tasks leading to 100% scheduling effectiveness with zero mission deviations

- oversaw all cash operations, disbursing more than $55.5M in military and travel pay vouchers

- oversaw eight crucial functional check flights to validate...

- oversaw force protection for 50 job sites in a 10 square mile area of responsibility enabling...

- oversaw the storage and delivery of $5M in...annually for...

- participated in every major contingency operation to include ENDURING FREEDOM and...

- participated in the distribution of over...to DoD treatment facilities worldwide

- performed at Division-level in supervisor role for critical...support and planning

- performed successful equipment deployment extending the BGM-109 Tomahawk's longevity into 2015

- performed over 500 hours RWP at a 98% on-time completion rate...

- phenomenal control of items allowed...

- played a key role in reaching several milestones

- prepared unit for real world deployments in...

- preserved 1200 vital assets

- preserved on-time delivery for over 1,000...in support of...

- processed an average of 1500 military pay documents monthly with a 99% accuracy rate

- produced a 100% pass rate for...

- professionalism and dedication to duty produced lasting contributions to Patrol and Reconnaissance Wing TWO

- protected 5 billion dollars in war assets

- protected Navy circuits from outside malicious logic attacks

- proved invaluable during three arduous and extended combat deployments to...

- proved to be an invaluable asset for the entire division

- proven leader under fire and a superior NCO

- provided assistance for the annual Expeditionary Warfare Training deployment

- provided continuous proactive solutions ensuring the availability of non-expendable, durable, and expendable supplies and equipment

- provided critical logistical support to the organization by timely management of personnel and equipment worth in excess of $100,000 with 0% loss of man hours

- provided critical support to the...

- provided essential computer and communication systems to personnel deployed to...

- provided exceptional maintenance critical to the completion of over 5,500 combat reconnaissance missions

- provided exceptional managerial acumen, critical to the completion of over 200...

- provided exceptional supply support to forces directly engaging terrorist networks within Afghanistan

- provided extraordinary support to units on...

- provided flawless Forward Operating Base support for 5 STS and 15 EELV missions

- provided leadership and direction for the shop

- provided maintenance support for a vehicle fleet of over 1000 vehicles

- provided much needed guidance and supervision during...

- provided over half a million meals served with zero customer complaints

- provided quality assurance oversight of a $15 million ship maintenance contract including...

- provided safe and reliable transportation to...

- provided timely support and replacements to over 5,000 deployed troops in two AORs

- provided vital oversight of over $90 million of C3 plus up equipment throughout the...

- published over 500 frequency authorizations and mission packages and...

- quickly adapted to changing circumstances, short lead times to...

- recognized for unfailing support to...

- registered and screened well over 2,500 personnel...

- remarkable technical ability prevented circuit or equipment downtime during...

- repeatedly exemplified dedication to his unit, the Fleet, and the Navy by...

- represented the U.S. Navy in an exemplary manner

- resilience and energy demonstrated by infallible delivery of...

- responsible for a sustained 95% mission-capable rate which helped earn the Norfolk Best Vehicle Maintenance Unit of the Year Award

- resulted in 100% compliance of all Command and unit requirements ensuring all Sailors are worldwide deployable

- resulted in minimal down time

- resulted in zero security incidents

- safe guarded 300 transient personnel this year

- safeguarded 10 million dollars in base infrastructure to...

- safeguarded flight safety of 50,000 air operations yearly

- secured an emergency back-up capability in place for...

- service contributed to successful accomplishment of...

- set an excellent example for his subordinates by demanding excellence and respect at the same time

- shaped 90% maintenance pass rate

- showed unparalleled and repeated initiative and tenacity

- significant contributions propelled LPD 9 to best in Navy honors as winners of the 2009 Battle Effectiveness Award

- single-handedly managed the Family Care Plans for thirty department members

- spent countless hours ensuring that his assigned vehicle system was in top condition and...

- spent countless hours fulfilling equipment and uniform needs of deploying Sailors

- stellar leadership and dedication to duty were vital to the movement of cargo and passengers on...

- strengthened overseas contingency operations in support of the Global War on Terror

- succeeded in having his section maintain support for...

- successfully executed base defense patrols, aggressive defense measures, and armed mobile responses to contribute significantly to the safety and security of...

- successfully led the risk management program for the...

- superb management skills ensured serviceable...

- superior analytical and technical capabilities facilitated the...

- superior and unyielding service to the...

- superior sustained performance proved invaluable to...

- supervised 15 personnel to ensure the integrity of...

- supervised over 150 emergency response personnel from 15 agencies, integrating and focusing their efforts to...

- supported expeditionary forces at Sigonella Air Station, Italy and Naval Station Rota, Spain

- supported more than 550 high visibility missions

- supported Naval Air Station Jacksonville Fuel Division through his strong commitment to maintenance

- sustained a robust and effective system help desk

- sustained the busiest...

- Systems Watch cited as superb and "fastest response time seen to date!"

- teamed with Command Stock Control to ensure accurate stock levels were loaded cutting cannibalization rate to 1%

- technical expertise and leadership played a direct role in...

- technical expertise in...proved invaluable during the...

- the dedication of...was key to the success of...

- the efforts expended during 2009 as a manager and Resource Advisor garnered him the...

- the extraordinary leadership of Chief Petty Officer Smith was instrumental in managing...

- the force behind the maintenance of $2 million in network infrastructure which...

- the perpetual efforts of YN1 Smith contributed to the overall mission in support of...

- though meticulous maintenance practice and preparation, she...

- through his commitment to excellence and expertise, he led a team to achieve 100% accountability of...

- throughout his assignment, HM2 Smith provided immediate medical care and aided in the stabilization of patients until higher medical care was available

- throughout the deployment, supervised over 150 Sailors and oversaw the movement of more than 5,000 passengers and 150,000 tons of cargo

- tireless dedication to duty contributed immeasurably to the many successes of the Fleet

- took great pride in the care and upkeep of his assigned equipment

- tracked and rectified monthly expenditures within an $55,000 budget

- tracked and managed over $550 million in construction projects throughout...

- triumphant! Directed maintenance of more than 50 diverse vehicles

- trusted in vital capacity as...

- under his command and direction the...

- under his guidance, 75% of the division acquired and maintained excellent or good fitness scores

- under threat of rocket and mortar attack, Petty Officer Smith...

- unflagging efforts facilitated the movement of 5,500 passengers and over 1,500 square feet of cargo

- unmatched diagnostic abilities and expert repairs directly sustained a 95% mission capable rate

- unparalleled in primary duties

- utilized his 15 years of experience, ensured the unit excelled during...

- versatile Sailor, quickly adapted to changing requirements and short lead times

- vital to successful operations

- was directly responsible for the effectiveness of a 15 member team through all mission phases with 100% success

- was essential to the squadron's overall "Excellent" inspection rating

- was exceptionally responsive and accurate while responding to over 50 intrusions alarms

- was instrumental in the completion of over 1,000 job orders valued at over $250,000 while 50% manned...

- was solely responsible for...

- when an emergency left the...position vacant, he quickly and fearlessly stepped into the demanding role

- when the J6 NCOIC was deployed, ET1 Smith stepped up and took over the section

- whether supporting federal or military missions, he performed impeccably and without fail

- which ensured contingency operation skills were developed and honed

- with a vision of success, she established high expectations and standards, which directly contributed to...

- with earnest precision, he expertly managed the most critical operational missions assigned to...

- with precise expertise and flawless performance, directly contributed to the...recertification

- with zero mishaps and a 99% on-time reliability rate

- withstood inclement weather conditions and never gave up

- worked around the clock to...

- worked extensively on the internal and external training programs within the unit

- worked over 300 additional man hours putting his and other sections of the EOD Mobile Unit in order to facilitate EOD readiness

Write With Impact

Well written evaluations, whether for new recruits or Captains, have one thing in common: the accomplishments listed all have their positive result listed. When describing accomplishments in an eval, in order to communicate how resourceful or effective that work was, we have to state what the end result of the action was. Otherwise the reader may not realize or understand the significance of your achievements. Typically the work performed is listed first followed by the positive result. Example:

- ET1 Jones traced the failure to a faulty cable and replaced *restoring critical communications necessary for BALTOPS 09 command*

The statements in the eval *must* communicate a beneficial result for every statement made. If, for some reason, you can't think of a beneficial result, try to connect the statement to something that *is* remarkable. Examples:

- He supervised 13 Sailors in the medical support of the Camp Dwyer flightline construction project which produced the largest expeditionary airfield in Marine Corps history.

- He marshaled the ship's Self Defense Force of 2 gun boats with which he secured and exerted coalition control over two oil platforms producing $10,000,000 of oil a day.

Below are examples of impacts or positive results.

- $1.6 billion in resources secured
- 100% compliant!
- 100% succcess
- 50% increase in on- time rates
- 95% on- time completion rate, smashed NAVEUR 90% goal
- a 50% reduction in required training time
- a readiness rate exceeding Navy goal by 5%
- a 99% accuracy rate
- a historical milestone
- a squadron first!
- a sustained 95% mission-capable rate
- a vital component during semi- annual assessment
- accelerated delivery of over $15 million worth of projects
- accomplished all learning objectives in 50% less...
- achieved "Most Improved Lodging" recognition
- achieved 100% accountability of...
- achieved a 5.5 average customer rating which exceeded goal
- actions landed "best nuclear engineer" award
- actions were imperative to mission success
- activated network supporting Joint Expeditionary Force
- advanced the warfare planning tool by two full years
- aided 5 deliveries of over 150K lbs of aid directly to...
- aided immeasurably in section's performance during...
- alleviated manning shortage at...
- allowed staff to make rapid manning decisions regarding...
- allowed immediate resumption of supply requests
- amassed over 1000 hours of instruction and...
- an invaluable asset for the entire unit

- an outstanding 100% uptime rate
- and prevented threat to the installation
- assisted in coping with multiple conflicts
- assisted Fleet's earning a rating of "Excellent"
- assured an atmosphere of mutual trust and respect
- assured successful event coverage
- at no cost to unit
- average turnaround 48 hrs
- averted an alert aircraft tail swap
- avoided an engine replacement cost of $900k
- avoided loss or cancellation of over $50M of year end funds
- awarded "Sailor of the Month" every month deployed
- beat repair estimate by over 12 hours!
- became the "gold standard" for other Navy programs
- bolstered operations in...
- boosted equipment to the next level of acquisition
- boosted section repair capabilities
- boosted squadron morale
- bridged the Supply Chain Management support gap
- broke record in maintenance response time
- brought program back on track
- built and maintained unit morale
- capitalized on emerging circumstances!
- captured an impressive 15 trophies and seized Best Team
- cemented a 100% pass rate
- certified over 55 firefighters with zero accidents to date
- chosen to manage distinguished visitor events for...
- cited as superb and "fastest response time seen to date!"

- clarified vital technical procedures
- clearly exceeded command standard of 95% accuracy
- close coordination ensured all equipment was...
- coined by Commander for his outstanding work in...
- collected in excess of $5,500 for the American Red Cross
- commended by staff for his efforts
- completed 100 deployment taskings in support of...
- completed all mission phases with 100% success
- completed in less than six months!
- completed ahead of schedule
- completed systematic audit with zero discrepancies
- completed well ahead of deadline
- completion rate in Navy's top 5%
- contributed immeasurably to the Fleet's many successes
- contributed significantly to the safety and security of...
- contributed significantly to the success of...
- controlled accuracy and locked in 100% accountability of...
- cost avoidance of $155K and involved in project's success
- created a positive environment for all members of...
- crucial to weapons safety training for...
- cultural relationship maintained
- cut the delinquent rate by 70%
- decisiveness saved $55M aircraft and 2 aircrew members
- decreased the risk of...
- delinquency rates plummeted 50%
- delivered 100% accurate accountability of all N3 assets
- delivered over $15M in base infrastructure improvements
- delivered over 550,000 pounds of presents to...

- delivered products within a never before seen two days
- delivered under budget and ahead of schedule
- deployed a Joint Task Force into a combat environment
- deployed three times ISO OEF/OIF/HOA
- designated Distinguished Graduate and recipient of the...
- deterred enemy attacks and safeguarded...
- developed self- discipline and confidence
- directly contributed to 155 enemy targets destroyed
- directly contributed to the success and achievements of...
- directly enabled evacuation of 155 patients, delivery of...
- directly improved combat medic capabilities and...
- directly responsible for the high level of readiness
- directly supported the ship's 555 accident-free hours
- disbursed more than $55M in military and travel pay
- discovered and corrected more than 550 errors
- distributed over 7k tons of relief supplies to Haitians
- donated over 150 hours during non-duty days
- dramatically improved Navy Expeditionary Training
- dual certified by the Navy and the state of Florida
- earned distinction as Master...
- earned the DOD Best Anti-terrorism Program for 2009
- earned the respect of subordinates
- earned twelve college credits, completed over six hours of...
- effectively ensured flight deck safety
- efficient delivery and smooth transition to deployment ops
- eliminated 30 days downtime and saved over $5,000 in...
- eliminated countless man hours of manual processing
- eliminated hazards in 30 critical facilities

- eliminated need for additional finance briefings
- eliminated parts order and mission delay
- elite mentor and manager
- emulated by all who know him
- enabled a vital lifeline between convoys
- enabled coalition forces to...
- enabled delivery of essential medical supplies to...
- enabled deployed warriors to focus on mission
- enabled on-time medications for over 5,000 customers
- enabled secure comm and emergency landing clearance
- enabled successful transfer of mission to PACOM
- ended a chronic 6 month work backlog
- enforced anti-terrorism protocols, ensured readiness
- enhanced and improved the overall state of unit readiness
- enhanced compliance with INSURV requirements
- enhanced survival capabilities
- enhanced upgrade training
- ensured $250K of equipment spared from destruction
- ensured 100% accountability of all N6 assets located on...
- ensured 100% compliance
- ensured 100% record accountability and evaluation
- ensured 100% serviceability
- ensured all members were worldwide deployable
- ensured the rapid evacuation of over 15,000 US citizens
- ensured the safety of over 1,000 deployed personnel
- ensured the security of over...
- ensured uninterrupted services to all users
- ensured zero penalties were incurred

- epitomized the trait of tenaciousness
- essential to the success of the Fleet's mission
- essential to unit's "Excellent" rating
- established a center of excellence for aspiring leaders
- established a comprehensive program for evolving...
- established critical programs including dependent care
- exceeded all expectations
- exceeded DISAEUR goal by 50%
- exceeded written requirements and led to recognition by...
- excelled as key planner during deployment
- excelled in a demanding role
- excelled in his duties as...
- excellent work ethic
- exceptional accuracy
- exceptional maintenance ability!
- exceptional oversight of 20 individual file plans
- executed 15K work orders on time/on target
- exemplified dynamic management
- exemplified the highest standards of commitment
- exhibited extraordinary service
- exhibited thorough knowledge of...
- expanded services to approximately 155 facilities
- expanded the capabilities of his section through...
- expanded the combat bed down capacity by 50%
- extended the lifespan of $30M system by two years
- facilitated 155 major emergency medical evacuations
- facilitated critical delivery of...
- facilitated delivery of more than 55,000 tons of cargo

- facilitated the movement of 5,500 passengers and...
- facilitated the acquisition of...
- fielded critical system which mitigated threat to...
- filled in the gaps of our experience, multiplied effectiveness
- finalized plans for successful transition to...
- first responder to Somali attack, aid critical
- forged partnership with...
- forged promising relationship with...
- fostered a "total force" vision
- fostered a positive environment
- fostered open, candid, and frequent communications
- gained the trust and respect of Sailors and leaders at...
- garnered a 95.5% mission capable rate
- garnered unwavering respect of team
- garnered widespread recognition
- generated $155,000 in lodging income
- generated a 95% ready rate
- great support!
- greatly improved equipment accountability and aided in...
- greatly improved morale of...
- greatly improved workcenter efficiency
- guaranteed mission readiness
- guaranteed safe deployment of...
- guaranteed the success of...
- guided contracting team to successful resolution
- handled all aspects of...
- helped 15 Sailors pass their fitness tests
- helped earn the COMSUBGRU 7 Unit of the Year Award

- helped reduce budget
- helped secure win of COMPACFLT Effectiveness Award 09
- huge effort!
- identified, recovered over $5,000 worth of reparable assets
- impeccable ethical and moral standards
- improved accuracy by nearly 100% at three bases in...
- improved communications security handling
- improved Sailors' overall system comprehension
- improved combat readiness of over 150 security personnel
- improved J3 continuity of operations preparedness
- improved productivity and morale of the mechanics
- improved scores from poor to good categories in 6 months
- improved their quality of life
- in-commission rate consistently better than Navy standard
- increased bulk storage
- increased CENTCOM intelligence, surveillance, and...
- increased communications access by an amazing 500%
- increased efficiency and safety of Task Force vehicles
- increased equipment reliability, reduced service calls
- increased patronage by 200%
- increased productivity
- increased the safety and efficiency of...
- increased service to 2,000 military members
- increased support to field organizations
- inducted into Fuel Section's elite "One Million Gallon Club"
- influenced Suicide Prevention success, raised contact...
- innovation made her a recognized expert in...
- instrumental in the successful closure of...

- instrumental in the unit receiving an excellent rating
- instrumental to the continued nuclear survivability of...
  instrumental in the ship's success in...
- integral member of planning committee
- integral to the success of 155 stellar performances
- integrated doctrine and policy into contingency operations
- integrated information from multiple intelligence platforms
- investigated/closed over 500 pay problems in less than...
- kept critical system temperature control for missile defense
- kept high demand ISR assets airborne 98% of the time
- kept the error rate to less than 1%
- key to overall effectiveness and success of...
- key to the survival of more than 150 wartime casualties
- laid foundation for effective integration and strategic focus
- lauded by team chief as "outstanding performer"
- launched long-needed program
- led to 100% scheduling effectiveness with zero deviations
- led to systemic changes that were applied command-wide
- made sure systems were up to date and combat ready
- maintained 100% accountability of 500 classified assets
- maintained a 95% in-commission rate
- maintained a 97% fill rate crushing the standard of 85%
- maintained a constant combat-ready posture
- maintained an outstanding 99% accuracy rate
- maintained an effective chain of command while deployed
- major influence on the effectiveness of unit's program
- minimal down time!
- minimized the amount of unserviceable equipment on...

- mitigated equipment downtime, saved the Fleet over $1M
- no mission capability lapse
- obtained 100% of the inspection points possible
- often singled out as the best in Second Fleet
- on-time rate of 95%
- organized over 5,500...
- outstanding and reliable Team Chief
- outstanding work orders were improved by 90%
- over 3K arrivals/departures on same ramp without incident
- oversight was critical in construction of support facilities
- perimeter defense maintained at crucial moments
- positively impacted contingency operations
- potentially saved the Navy more than...
- prepared Force members for future leadership roles
- prepared 500 multi-service warriors in support of...
- prepared ABM students for...
- prepared for the largest mass deployment since 2007
- prepared senior leadership to defend future Fleet...
- prepared unit for real world deployments
- preserved 1200 vital assets
- prevented a $125,000 stock fund adjustment and loss
- prevented a major emergency and loss of life
- prevented circuit or equipment downtime during...
- prevented elimination of $5B in future FY budgets
- prevented failures and guaranteed full compliance with...
- prevented sizeable force structure reductions
- procured free resources saving the Navy over $500K
- produced an overall increase in productivity Fleet wide

- produced a phenomenal 100% pass rate
- produced equipment within an unheard of two day notice
- project completed under budget, funds diverted to...
- promoted good will among coalition partners
- propelled VP-47 to best in Navy honors as winner of...
- protected $5 billion worth of Protection Level 1 resources
- protected Navy circuits from outside malicious logic
- proved himself a true total force warrior
- proved world-wide capability
- proven ability!
- proven leader under fire and a superior NCO
- provided 1500 hours of continuous, crucial service
- provided a year and a half of flawless customer service
- provided accurate information for all levels of leadership
- provided critical input to Commander and staff
- provided relief to the devastated country of...
- provided unprecedented air control architecture for...
- put five aircraft back into service within 3 days instead of...
- qualified 15 watch members in Advanced Intel Training
- raised $6,000 in the first week, well beyond the goal of...
- raised equipment availability 55%
- raised the accuracy of...
- raised the level of force protection
- re-energized the fire training program
- ready for real world deployments
- received letter of appreciation for celebrated holiday meal
- recognized as Sailor of the Year for 2009
- recognized as an exemplary program

- recognized as Knuckle Buster for 2nd Quarter
- recognized as top performer
- recouped $55K of units' funds
- reduced accident rate by 60%
- reduced amount of assets on-site, still met mission!
- reduced cargo footprint by 50%
- reduced Cat 1 errors by 50%
- reduced check-in process time by 50%
- reduced duplication and processing errors by 10%
- reduced error rate 5% below Defense standard of 12%
- reduced monetary demand on FY 10 budget
- reduced unit backlog by...
- reduced wait by 50%
- removed threat, protected base populace
- rendered building secure
- rendered the surrounding community a safer place
- repaired perimeter fence breach in less than 5 hours
- repeatedly exemplified dedication to the Fleet and the Navy
- rescued floundering program from evolving budget lapse
- resolved a three year inventory void
- resolved critical radio frequency interference issues
- responsible for successful launches of...
- restored critical power to during two widespread outages
- resulted in a 100% pass rate
- resulted in a 100% replacement of laptop computers
- resulted in accreditation in all areas
- resulted in the first-ever bilateral information conference
- resulted in zero losses or injuries for deployed personnel

- resulting in minimal down time
- returned $50,000 of assets to supply system
- returned 100% of equip from Joint Base to home station
- returned to Fully Mission Capable 5 days ahead of schedule
- reutilized excess parts, saved Navy $50,000
- revitalized training within the Weapons Instructor Course
- revived failing First Class association
- safeguarded 300 transient personnel
- safeguarded 10 million dollars in base infrastructure
- safeguarded 500 Sailors and facilities worth over $155M
- safely removed dangerously unsafe munitions
- saved $1,500 in labor and replacement costs and averted...
- saved $550,000 in maintenance and certification fees
- saved the lives of over 50 patients
- saved user many hours of lost productivity
- seamlessly implemented new course revisions
- seamlessly integrated with on-site personnel
- section qualified 100% go on certifications
- secured an "Outstanding" rating for the Ship
- secured over 3,000 dollars for...
- seized the 2009 NAVEUR Small Unit of the Year award
- selected as the Senior NCO of the 1st and 2nd quarter 2009
- set the example for fellow shipmates to follow
- shaped evolving Command and Control plans for...
- slashed the standard 3 month training window to only...
- smashed JMAST standard of one week per...
- smashed the twelve hour standard
- solely responsible for expedient recovery

- solidified comm support to ensure operational safety
- spurred a 25% increase in productivity
- stabilized life threatening condition
- standardized policies for a 12 nation consortium
- strengthened contingency operations in support of...
- strengthened relations between Navy and host nation
- success guaranteed!
- successfully deployed with no complications
- successfully targeted four high-value targets
- supported members and veterans in need
- supported over 500 personnel in operations spanning...
- sustained 95% mission capable rate which helped earn...
- sustained an impressive 95% maintenance departure rate
- sustained and reestablished operations
- task completion 72 hours ahead of headquarters deadline
- the most significant recognition ever awarded
- the preeminent operational and training expert
- touched lives of less fortunate
- twice recognized as NCO of the Quarter
- united diverse team and increased efficiency
- unlimited talent!
- unmatched diagnostic abilities
- unparalleled leadership
- unparalleled safety improvement
- vital to mission success and crew integrity
- vital to training of 15 fellow Network Administrators
- well prepared for potential cut-over of all operations
- were prepared for deployment

- which produced an EXCELLENT for unit fitness program
- which was lauded by General Patton as...
- won 2010 Sailor of the Year for...
- workcenter won Certificate of Excellence
- zero customer complaints
- zero discrepancies during the base staff assistance visit
- zero errors
- zero mishaps
- zero mission interruptions
- zero security incidents

Positive Adjectives

In order to present as positive a picture as possible of the person being evaluated, adjectives should be chosen carefully and should fit the situation. Below are examples of positive adjectives appropriate for most evals.

above average	ambitious
acclaimed	analytical
accomplished	articulate
active	assured
adaptable	astute
adept	attentive
admirable	authoritative
advanced	aware
advancing	
aggressive	balanced
agile	beneficial
alert	best

bold

brave

bright

brilliant

bulletproof

calm

capable

careful

cautious

certified

commanding

commendable

committed

compassionate

competent

confident

conscientious

conservative

considerate

consistent

contributing

cooperative

courageous

courteous

creative

critical

daring

decisive

dedicated

deliberate

dependable

detail-oriented

determined

diligent

diplomatic

discreet

dominating

driven

dutiful

dynamic

eager

earnest

educated

effective

efficient

eloquent

enabling

encouraging

energetic

energized

enterprising

enthusiastic

essential

excellent

exceptional

experienced

expert

facilitating

fair

faithful

fearless

firm

flawless

flexible

focused

forceful

genuine

goal-oriented

gung-ho

hard working

hard-charging

helpful

honorable

imaginative

impartial

important

impressive

independent

indispensable

industrious

inexhaustible

influential

informed

ingenious

innovative

insatiable

inspired

intelligent

invaluable

inventive

invested

involved

judicious

just

key

knowledgeable

lasting

leading

learned

level-headed

logical

loyal

masterful

mature

methodical

meticulous

modest

motivated

multi-skilled

multi-talented

nimble

no-nonsense

notable

observant

orderly

organized

out-standing

peerless

perceptive

perfect

persevering

persistent

persuasive

poised

polished

positive

practical

practiced

praiseworthy

precise

prepared

proactive

productive

professional

proficient

prominent

promising

protective

proven

prudent

punctual

qualified

quick

quick-thinking

rational

ready

reasonable

recognized

relentless

reliable

remarkable

reputable

resilient

resolute

resourceful

responsible

results-oriented

satisfactory

scrupulous

secure

selected

self-assured

self-confident

self-motivated

self-reliant

selfless

sensible

serious

sharp

significant

sincere

skillful/skilled

smart

sober

spirited

stable

stalwart

steadfast

steady

sterling

strong

sturdy

successful

superb

superior

supportive

sustaining

systematic

tactful

talented

tenacious

tested

thorough

thoughtful

tireless

top

tough

traditional

trained

trustworthy

wise

working

unfailing

unique

unlimited

unmatched

unrivaled

unstoppable

unsurpassed

valuable

veteran

vigilant

vigorous

vital

watchful

well-grounded

willing

Opening Comment Examples

The purpose and goal of the Eval is to accurately and fully describe performance. A laundry list of significant achievements does provide insight into a person's capabilities but it doesn't provide the whole picture. A list of achievements doesn't give any indication as to the character or personality of the person being evaluated. A Sailor might have a long list of impressive accomplishments but, at the same time, be a discipline problem and hard to work with. He or she might be an expert in their rating but the absolute worst at sharing knowledge or getting along with their peers or subordinates. And those social qualities are very important, at least as important as a person's technical skills. So, in addition to describing a person's professional and technical skills, we need to convey to the Eval's reader his social skills, his integrity, his character, his loyalty and other qualities which are not apparent when merely reading a list of accomplishments. The Opening statements or comments is where this facet of performance is described. This statement is very important. It's the first thing the reader sees and sets the tone for the whole Eval. Make sure it has the impact that can't be ignored.

#1 of four Chief Petty Officers! An outstanding leader and top performer who delivered stellar results during the Global War on Terrorism.

#1 of seven planners! Successfully trained dozens of theater watch officers and was vital to USJFCOM/COMSECONDFLT mission success.

***ALTHOUGH 1 OF 1, THIS PO1 SHOULD BE FAST
TRACKED TO CPO!***

**MY # 4 OF 15 OUTSTANDING CPOs ASSIGNED TO ACU-
2 SEA COMPONENT**

A capable and dedicated Petty Officer, he always exercises
sound judgment and has displayed strong leadership
potential. Continuously reviews actions and strives for
improvement of his section. Groom for future position of
responsibility.

A dynamic and highly motivated leader. Aggressively tackled
the most demanding assignments, completing them with
exceptional results. Outstanding leadership, managerial
skills, and an unusually high level of professional
competence have contributed significantly to the unit's high
state of readiness.

A first-rate Petty Officer who is willing to face up to any task
and tackle the issues head on.

A leader with an indefatigable work ethic. Hand-picked to be
the only E-7 to attain the title of Senior Watch Officer which
is usually held by an E-8. He makes the process of managing
the Ops Center look easy.

A Self-Starter whose personal initiative and leadership skills
guarantee exceptional results of all tasks assigned. Specific
accomplishments include:

A superb Second Class Petty Officer. Versatile and
exceptionally productive. Petty Officer Smith's skill in
merging textbook knowledge with personal "hands on"
experience makes him the premier technician in his rate and
an ideal role model. His tireless work ethic instills a high

level of unity and professional pride in the workcenter. Specific accomplishments include:

A task-oriented, conscientious SCPO whose efforts led to increased workcenter efficiency and effectiveness.

A true professional. Produces accurate and timely results. His computer and network expertise was sought daily by peers and supervisors throughout the ship.

A truly outstanding Second Class Petty Officer. His potential for positions of higher authority is unlimited. Demonstrates unfailing diligence, aggressiveness, and total dedication to duty. Thoroughly prepared for every assignment.

A truly superb Second Class Petty Officer. Highly knowledgeable, intensely motivated, and dedicated. Leads with ease and confidence inspiring subordinates to perform at their peak capability. Possesses the technical ability to excel at any task. Continually seeks additional tasks and responsibility. Specific accomplishments include:

A welcome new addition to the Power Generation workcenter, Petty Officer Gonzalez is a Sailor with promise. Although still in training, volunteered for and excelled as:

Absolute TOP NOTCH in every respect. The only E-6 to attain the title of Senior Watch Officer, a leader in whom I place extraordinary trust!

Absolutely superior Petty Officer; excelled in job performance, community service, and leadership. Early Promote.

Absolutely TOP NOTCH sailor! Efficient and perceptive CIC Watch Supervisor! Managed a seasoned watch team responsible for defense of ship and personnel. He created an atmosphere of trust and cooperation and coordinated efforts of key personnel to establish interlocking redundancy and teamwork; promises survival and success; best CIC in 2nd Fleet!

Although a new addition to the department, Seaman Smith has displayed an insatiable interest for learning about his rate and the military.

An excellent leader, manager, and organizer. Performs at the highest caliber in every endeavor. His "lead by example" style ensures only the highest quality work from his subordinates. Demonstrated innovative and independent thinking as well as cooperation. Complete technical understanding enables him to react quickly and with versatility to changing priorities.

An excellent performer; always looks for ways to improve the working environment for the DDG-96 USS Bainbridge team.

An Outstanding Second Class Petty Officer. Continually sets the example for others to follow. An exceptional leader and manager who instills enthusiasm and pride in subordinates. Skillfully formulates solutions to complex maintenance tasks and has won the confidence of seniors and subordinates alike.

An outstanding Second Class Petty Officer. Efficient, industrious, and conscientious. Continually projects the highest degree of professionalism, enthusiasm, and motivation. Specific accomplishments include:

An outstanding First Class Petty Officer. Petty Officer Smith is a highly motivated individual who performs every task with determination and devotion. His commitment to

90

excellence and "can do" spirit are unequaled. A self-starter who sets the pace for others to follow. Initiative and leadership skills guarantee exceptional results in any endeavor.

As Chief of the Boat, he is a superior leader whose innate ability to motivate, inspire, and train personnel significantly improved productivity and command performance.

As Tech Control LPO, CTM1 Smith has demonstrated his maturity as an exceptional deckplate leader and motivator. He consistently sets competitive goals for his team and provides the necessary guidance to help them reach them.

Chief Petty Officer Smith is an outstanding leader and manager. Consistently superior performer. Totally dedicated to mission accomplishment. Intelligent, charismatic team player with natural ability to inspire civilian and military personnel. Unlimited potential.

Chief Petty Officer Smith's enthusiastic performance in every endeavor has been of the highest caliber. He is an invaluable manager, counselor, and source of knowledge in all technical areas.

Chief Jones is the clear leader of my department who makes excellence look routine. Has the rare ability to anticipate and prepare for the unexpected. Exceptional planner who runs my watch with the class and vision of a much senior Chief Petty Officer.

CPO Jones is an enthusiastic, dedicated CPO. She has quickly transitioned from a maintenance background to her new staff duties and embraced her new challenges with vigor.

Deckplate leadership at its finest! Marked P only due to short time on board and quota restraints. Stellar leadership and exceptional mastery of tactical and technical skills. Clear front-runner for Chief.

Demonstrated outstanding engineering skills and maturity. Exceeded standards in a complex and dynamic environment.

Dependable, motivated, and trustworthy; an LPO with the courage to manage without visible support.

Enthusiastic and dedicated, actively seeks out challenges and doggedly pursues them until resolved. He is singled out for jobs that require determination and skill and has improved or corrected many chronic problem areas. He is a shining example to his peers and subordinates.

Enthusiastic, thorough, and curious, has unmatched interest and capacity for learning. Possesses a strong sense of pride in service and self-discipline and is a model Petty Officer. Can be counted on, even under the most austere circumstances, to complete any task assigned.

ET1 Jones, a graduate of Advanced Engineering course and a career-long engineer, knows this platform like the back of his hand and enjoys the challenge of serving aboard a ship with a reputation for being the most difficult to support.

Excellent technical abilities; motivated and self-confident seaman; consistently performs high quality work.

Exceptional First Class Petty Officer. Innovative, motivated, and conscientious. Demonstrated a sincere and personal concern in his work with students, assisting them with career and advancement information and studies.

First-class PO whose can-do attitude and ceaseless determination are contagious. An excellent role model.

GM1 Smith is head and shoulders above his peers and the finest E6 I've ever known. He functions as a CPO every single day- the only thing missing are the anchors!

Good work ethic; tackles any task above his skill level with outstanding results. Promotion to E-6 recommended.

Highly motivated! Energetic and diligent; demonstrated strong ability to identify, analyze, and solve problems.

Highly motivated and an indispensable member of the team. She is routinely sought out by junior technicians for advice and counseling.

Highly motivated and determined to succeed in his job. Completes all tasks correctly first time; an indispensable member of the department.

Highly reliable and key team member. He is well trained, has years of experience across multiple platforms, and is knowledgeable on all spectrums of satellite equipment.

Highly skilled and dedicated professional, performs far beyond expectations; an invaluable asset and vital to Navy mission.

IT1 Smith has been a valuable asset to the EUCOM J6 directorate while deployed to Patch Barracks, Stuttgart, Germany in support of the GWOT. He was hand-picked for a critical and arduous deployment to Kosovo to supervise operations there.

IT1 Smith has earned his reputation for skill and reliability; he impresses his peers and inspires his subordinates and I have entrusted him with the Fleet's most critical programs.

Most emphatically ready for Chief Petty Officer selection! Dedicated, motivated LPO, responsible for 22 personnel, she supervised the management and services at the SARP treatment facility flawlessly.

My #1 of 4 top notch Petty Officers. A proactive leader and exemplary Sailor who led the most active section in the squadron.

My #1 of 7 Petty Officers! Superior performance across the board. Give him bigger challenges and assign to our most critical positions!

My #1 Second Class Petty Officer without a doubt! Petty Officer Jones is an outstanding Storekeeper who epitomizes the Navy Core Values. He is an invaluable asset to the Bataan and the Navy Family. His dedication and relentless can-do attitude has had a significant impact on the ship's safety and technology support.

My best CIC Watch Supervisor! Developed and maintained an efficient and motivated watch characterized by professionalism and pride. PROMOTE TO CHIEF NOW!

My best CPO. Developed a hearty Chief's Mess that restored Navy tradition and pride. PROMOTE TO SCPO NOW!

My nominee for promotion under the Combat Meritorious Advancement Program. Promote this warrior now!

My number 2 of 4 extremely talented Petty Officers. Performance is indistinguishable from my #1. PROMOTE TO E-7 NOW!

Our most promising Senior Chief. SCPO Smith is the model of a successful Senior CPO in appearance, knowledge, and performance.

Outstanding and welcome addition to my CPO mess. In just 3 months he has made a huge impact on the CPO mess throughout DISA-EUR. Not ranked higher solely due to time onboard.

OUTSTANDING CPO who is scorching the competition. A true leader. Developed a cohesive Chief's Mess that focuses on the command's success. PROMOTE TO SCPO NOW!

Outstanding Petty Officer. Crisp military bearing and appearance. Exceeds standards in military courtesies, fitness, and job performance.

Outstanding and fearless Sailor with a can-do attitude. Always willing to take on more challenging tasks with greater responsibility.

Outstanding First Class Petty Officer. A born leader, who can be depended upon to share his experience. A talented and personable teacher, he constantly trained his subordinates in all aspects of the rating resulting in a lower error rate and higher morale in the workcenter.

Outstanding Second Class Petty Officer. Self-confident and versatile. Strong technical knowledge combined with aggressive leadership ability make him an effective performer and role model. Ability, attitude, and overall performance are the best in the department.

Petty Officer Smith, a veteran of numerous deployments, with over 13 years of experience, has provided indispensable leadership and guidance to our watch. His exemplary handling of administrative matters attests to his professional knowledge, willingness to accept responsibility, attention to detail, and the ability to adapt himself to any assignment or situation.

Petty Officer Smith's exceptional work ethic and devotion to duty contributed significantly to the accomplishment of the Command's mission of providing the best quality dental care to all eligible beneficiaries.

Petty Officer Jones is an exceptional Front Desk clerk whose performance exceeds all requirements. Intelligent and conscientious, he requires neither supervision nor guidance in order to attain superior results. His long term commitment to the improvement of his duties led to his selection as top Front Desk Clerk at the Combined Bachelors Quarters, Naval Station Pearl Harbor.

Petty Officer Smith is the Electrical and Troubleshooters Branch's proven technician. Superb leader. Very reliable and totally dedicated. Junior personnel continually look to him for guidance because of his keen insight and system knowledge.

Petty Officer Smith brings an enthusiasm and interest in his duties that make him a highly valued member of the security team. He goes out of his way to complete assigned tasks ahead of schedule and to support the team's future goals toward readiness.

Petty Officer Gonzalez consistently performed his demanding duties in an exemplary and highly professional manner. His exceptional work ethic and tenacity in direct support of his shipmates through the most difficult of mission taskings illustrate his remarkable commitment and dedication.

Petty Officer Smith has been a mainstay of the Operations department who makes himself continuously available to provide any required assistance. His professional knowledge and sound judgment, combined with his ability to work without supervision and his willingness to work beyond normal duty hours, evoked many favorable comments from the staff.

Petty Officer Jones is an energetic, proven performer and motivated Second Class Petty Officer. His boundless passion for the Navy inspires subordinates to produce quality results and is the cornerstone of our training program.

PO1 Smith is a consummate manager and master of his trade. With little support, he stood up the NMCB armory in less than 30 days and brought it into compliance with Naval standards, OPNAVIST instructions and USMC directives.

Petty Officer Smith is a highly motivated Sailor who is dedicated to not only improving himself, but encourages both junior and senior shipmates to strive for their best as well.

Petty Officer Smith is a driven and resourceful Second Class Petty Officer and outstanding technician. Can be relied upon to complete the most challenging assignments without direction or guidance. His no-nonsense leadership style is the foundation of the development of subordinates.

Petty Officer Smith is a supremely talented Second Class Petty Officer. He possesses an enthusiastic drive and determination in accomplishing the most demanding tasks.

Technically skilled. His dedicated workmanship greatly improved the operational readiness of squadron aircraft by providing aircrew with full mission capable weapon systems.

Petty Officer Smith is a proven technical expert and an indispensable leader within the Integrated Weapons Team. He inspires subordinates to mirror his peerless example of quality workmanship, safety, and commitment to excellence. Always maintains impeccable military bearing. Vigorously safeguards classified material in accordance with all applicable directives.

Petty Officer Smith is an exceptional administrator within the Fuels Branch. Possesses outstanding leadership skills. A true professional who is dedicated to the development of subordinates. Displays the maturity and self confidence of a seasoned Chief Petty Officer.

Petty Officer Jones is an inspirational leader with strong moral fiber who is respected by peers, subordinates, and superiors. A true professional in every sense of the word.

Petty Officer Smith is a superb Second Class Petty Officer and outstanding technician. Self-Motivated. Totally dedicated. Excels in every professional aspect. A hard charger who gets the job done every time regardless of complexity. Exemplary military bearing. Overall performance has been outstanding.

Petty Officer Smith is a superlative example of a Second Class Petty Officer. He is an ambitious self-starter who sustains a high level of motivation and resourcefulness in his performance.

Petty Officer Gonzalez is a top performer who possesses superb leadership abilities. Technical knowledge and experience enable him to excel wherever assigned. Tackles all tasks with confidence and a determination to succeed. Strongly supports command Equal Opportunity programs. Ensures compliance with all classified material handling directives.

Petty Officer Gonzalez is a dedicated Fire Control professional with a knack for being in the right place at the right time. His exceptional operational ability combined with his sound recommendations for the adoption of new techniques and more productive methods aided his unit in achieving and maintaining a high level of operational efficiency.

Petty Officer Gonzalez is a detail-oriented, driven First Class with outstanding communication skills and proven success interfacing with seniors and subordinates. He consistently operates at the Chief Petty Officer caliber!

Petty Officer Smith is a dominant performer with unlimited potential. His demonstration of a strong, functional knowledge of Front Desk responsibilities has resulted in his rapid qualification as Front Desk Clerk. CS3 Smith's ability to achieve optimal levels of personal achievement led to his nomination for Sailor of the Quarter.

Petty Officer Jones is always ready to respond to requests for service and goes above and beyond in delivering top flight results. His unusual ability and constant devotion to duty earned him the respect and admiration of all those with whom he served and contributed materially to the high standard of logistical support provided by Norfolk to the United States Joint Forces Command.

Petty Officer Smith is an average Second Class Petty Officer. He is willing to take charge when directed. All assigned tasks are completed in a safe and methodical manner. He is mission oriented and communicates well with others. Appearance on and off duty is above standards.

Petty Officer Jones is a motivated Petty Officer with a positive attitude and willingness to accept any assignment.

Petty Officer Smith is an extraordinary Aviation Ordnanceman and outstanding Second Class Petty Officer. An exceptional leader, manager, and organizer with endless ability.

Petty Officer Smith is an extremely knowledgeable and dedicated Aviation Storekeeper. Consistently surpassed all expectations. Customer service attitude contributed fully to work center's high morale and team spirit. A versatile individual who performs well in any type environment.

Petty Officer Smith is an indispensable leader and proven technician within the Integrated Weapons Team Branch. He is extremely well organized, mission oriented, and industrious. Aggressively tackles all tasks with utmost professionalism and tireless dedication. A true team player.

Petty Officer Jones is an essential member of our team who has distinguished himself through sustained superior performance. He is a dedicated professional who tackles the most demanding tasks with superior results. Promotes the total team concept. His keen rating knowledge and quality workmanship is the cornerstone for the training of junior personnel.

Petty Officer Jones is a full time professional that is noted for his ability to always get the job done right. His initiative, resourcefulness, and untiring efforts to achieve perfection in all phases of his duties as Systems Controller resulted in increased operational efficiency of the section.

Petty Officer Smith is a vital member of our department and a proven technician within the Branch. Highly reliable and dedicated, his quality workmanship and commitment to excellence is the cornerstone of our maintenance effort. Accepts only the highest quality of maintenance.

Petty Officer Smith is an industrious, conscientious, and highly motivated First Class who exhibits the highest degree of professionalism in accomplishing all tasks. Goal-oriented, he demonstrates a patient, relentless effort toward his assigned goals.

Petty Officer Smith is an OUTSTANDING Bottle Washer. Intelligent and versatile, he possesses in-depth knowledge and understanding of A-6 Bottle Washing Systems. He is determined to accomplish the most demanding tasks while providing superior results. Demonstrated strong, dynamic leadership exercising common sense and sound judgment in all circumstances. Maintains high standards of professional conduct and provides subordinates with constant support.

Petty Officer Smith is a gifted technician and a consistent top performer. He is agile and responsive to frequently changing operational requirements. Continuously provides quick, logical solutions to very difficult situations.

Petty Officer Smith is an outstanding LPO. Her aggressive leadership, attention to detail, and her lead by example style of leadership make her a vital asset to the unit's mission.

Petty Officer Smith is an outstanding technician who has proven himself, through sustained, superior performance, to be an asset to the command. Industrious, resourceful, and dedicated, he possesses limitless enthusiasm for his role as Security Officer.

Petty Officer Gonzalez is the TOP Second Class Petty Officer in my Command. An unparalleled Avionics technician with unsurpassed technical expertise, she thrives in the dynamic environment of carrier aviation. Her sterling professional example and leadership are the mainstay in the development of junior personnel.

Petty Officer Smith looks forward to providing the best customer service under all circumstances. His development of improved systems and procedures in the field of finance and accounting and in the supervision of their implementation represents a significant achievement.

Petty Officer Jones possesses a relentless need and ability to achieve. She is an intelligent, innovative leader who thrives on new challenges and transforms goals and objectives into concrete, workable plans.

Petty Officer Smith provides outstanding administrative support to the unit. He has demonstrated he has what it takes to keep the unit in order administratively. His skills and dedication are vital to the monthly rigors of the Naval Operational Support Center (NOLSC).

Petty Officer Smith readily accepts the most demanding duties and produces superior results. His tireless devotion to duty inspires and challenges co-workers.

Petty Officer Smith's performance since last reporting period is commendable. He is a resourceful Petty Officer who enjoys overcoming obstacles. Demonstrated enduring diligence and total dedication to duty. Willing to accept any assignment regardless of scope or difficulty.

Petty Officer Smith's performance, both militarily and professionally, is nothing short of outstanding. Displays keen interest in work. Contributes full measure to any task, willingly accepts added responsibility. He has my strongest possible recommendation for advancement to Petty Officer Second Class.

Petty Officer Jones' performance is nothing short of inspiring! Recruit poster appearance and military bearing. He won Blue Jacket of the 3rd Quarter 09.

Petty Officer Smith, in his short time here at VFA-2, has proven to be a fast learner in his duties and responsibilities as Assistant Security Manager. He is a motivated performer who shows promise and potential.

Petty Officer Smith thrives in the dynamic environment of carrier aviation. A fearless supervisor, she eagerly accepts all challenges, tackling them with thorough and well thought out planning. Demonstrated a pragmatic approach to managing and directing subordinates.

Petty Officer Smith, with over eight years experience, is in charge of our fuels management division and shouldered responsibility for numerous important initiatives. He maintained exemplary discipline and unit effectiveness. His mature leadership was key to the safe and efficient management and growth of the division.

Phenomenal Sailor; surpassed every expectation in training and duty performance; is overdue for promotion to Chief!

PO Smith is a highly skilled member and motivated Seaman; a valuable asset to the unit and the Navy's mission. Promote.

PO Smith is a top performer. Unlimited potential. Totally professional, poised, mature, and dedicated. He has consistently executed the weighty responsibilities of Watch Officer with fervor, determination, and overall success. Continually striving for personal growth, he rapidly quallfied as Watch Officer.

Petty Officer Smith is first-rate Yeoman who seizes every opportunity to excel. She has originated, routed, and stored our message traffic with 100% reliability and accuracy. Her diligence, combined with her talent for coordinating the complexities of contemporary administration, gave renewed impetus to the forms management and records administration programs of the Command.

PO1 Smith is a highly qualified Petty Officer who is directly responsible for an uptime rate of over 99% on all strategic communications links, exceeding stringent DISA standards.

PO1 Smith is an exceptional Petty Officer and capable leader who performed duties as jet engine mechanic in a professional manner.

PO2 Smith is a front runner whose performance has been consistently superb. His commitment to excellence and "can do" spirit are unequaled and has dramatically improved customer service. He consistently ensures all tasks are completed in an accurate and timely manner.

Petty Officer Smith demonstrated initiative, professional ability, and keen foresight in performing his duties in the logistics field. Through long-range planning and skillful oversight of the logistics program, he contributed immeasurably to the successful accomplishment of the Bainbridge mission.

Powerful right hand to the XO. Possessed an unsurpassed level of knowledge, organizational prowess, and a mature understanding of personnel dynamics and management. He expertly tracked all personnel and administrative actions under his watch with spectacular results.

Professional, methodical, and technically astute, FC2(SW) Smith consistently leads by example seeking greater responsibility while excelling at the most difficult tasks.

PROVEN ABILITY. I have observed him serving as Chief of the Boat, both at sea and in port, and his performance clearly demonstrates that he is ready now for assignment to this demanding billet.

Ranked # 1 of 5 highly competitive CPOs. Chief Smith is the most productive and versatile Chief at this Command. He has my complete confidence and is relied upon heavily for all vital network defense decisions for the USCENTCOM AOR.

Ranked #1 of 5 in Admin department and #4 of 10 assigned. An absolute must select for Chief Petty Officer.

Ranked #1 of 5 outstanding Petty Officers! Perfect combination of technical excellence and deckplate leadership. Promote to E-7 NOW!

Ranked #1 of 5 PO1s. Proven performance in a CPO billet. Makes my command better at every turn. Inspires subordinates to perform beyond expectations. Select now for CPO!

SCPO Jones is the epitome of a highly motivated Senior CPO in appearance, knowledge, and performance.

Senior Chief Petty Officer Smith's inspirational performance permeates my Command. The deep respect he receives from all hands is evidence of his superlative leadership qualities. His example has fostered unparalleled productivity and esprit de corps.

Senior Chief Smith reported onboard and immediately developed and executed a comprehensive improvement plan that turned a mediocre division into the best run ship's office on the pier.

SN Gonzalez has excellent technical abilities. A motivated and self-confident Sailor, she consistently performs high quality work.

SN Smith has stepped into the Patrol Division and quickly became an integral member of the duty section. Always willing to help and learn, he sets a great example for others to follow.

SN Jones is Third Division's top performer. Since taking over as leading SN, he has been nothing but full speed ahead. His ability to use the resources provided to him to complete all assigned tasks is unmatched. SN Smith is already performing at the Third Class Petty Officer level and is ready for the next challenge now.

Strong and dedicated performer. Displays the leadership ability of a top notch Petty Officer First Class.

Strong sense of responsibility and remarkable ability to plan, manage, and administer. Continually striving for personal growth, Petty Officer Smith has established himself as a valuable asset.

SUPERB CHIEF PETTY OFFICER! Hands-down my number one Chief Petty Officer in the mess! Energetic, dedicated leader whose performance always exceeds my highest expectations.

Superb performance across the board. Absolute professional, leader, and manager in all aspects. Exceptional technical knowledge and skill has greatly increased the operational excellence and capability of this squadron. A natural leader. Displays initiative and resourcefulness in all endeavors.

Superior leadership ability and command involvement earned him my top ranking. Number 1 of 6 outstanding Senior Chiefs. A natural leader. Selected over 14 other command E-7 and above personnel to fill short-fused OIC billet in Pearl Harbor Naval Station, Hawaii.

Superior performer. Dedicated and committed with unlimited leadership potential.

The second ranked Chief on board, Chief Smith is a model for the Navy's commitment to pride, professionalism, and personal excellence. Whatever the mission, he can be counted on to lead the winning team. Takes every task in stride, demonstrating daily that any job can be completed correctly, efficiently, and effectively.

This petty officer is enthusiastic, dedicated, and pays meticulous attention to detail. He eagerly accepts all assignments and is often chosen for tasks that require precision and maturity because he can be depended on to deliver stellar results.

This Petty Officer achieves optimal levels of performance & accomplishment with lasting results--PROMOTE TO CPO!

Top performer with unparalleled potential and solid CPO attributes; promote to Chief ahead of peers!

Top-notch technical abilities were key to mission success. Petty Officer Jones is ready for increased supervisory responsibility. Promote!

Trusted to oversee watch team responsible for defense of ship and personnel. He maintained an atmosphere of trust and cooperation and coordinated efforts of key personnel to establish interlocking redundancy and teamwork; promises survival and success; best CIC in 2nd Fleet!

YN1 Jones serves as administrative supervisor, keeps our day to day transactions in inspection-ready order, and is a vital part of our success. Through his keen personal interest, initiative, and untiring devotion to duty, YN1 Jones rendered invaluable assistance in the planning and execution of an improved Communications Security program.

Accomplishments

This section focuses on work-related bullet comments. The most effective eval statements are those that fully describe the accomplishment and, equally as importantly, describe the positive result of that action. The reason for this is that your eval will be read by Senior and Master Chiefs who know nothing about your job. They won't understand how significant your achievement is unless you tell them. In addition, make sure your statements describe actual, solid accomplishment and not just abstract ideas.

Remember: The eval's opening sentence or introduction is like the first sentence in a paragraph. The text you enter below it should support whatever assertions were made.

Example:

Petty Officer Smith's enthusiasm and mature work ethic have made him well-suited for the Material Control Division.
- He reorganized asset storage by department and frequency of use which reduced wait and allowed refueling and maintenance shops to expand their service rates.
- He devoted 25 off-duty hours to correct 3 major discrepancies that reduced equipment down time by 50%.

See the following pages for more examples of accomplishment-type bullet statements.

- 100% scrutiny of all message traffic kept center apprised of rapid changes and more informed than other fleet members. He has proven his ability to oversee the CIC in support of joint operations with allied navies.

- A diligent and tireless operator, he identified unobserved ship movements and approach which initiated mission generation and a successful diversion of threat and prevented loss to battle group.

- Aggressively coordinated over 50 subsistence deliveries valued at more than 500k for 12 foreign ships guaranteeing their continued successful exercise participation and improving joint operations skill.

- Always completed 100% of assigned tasks on time and her comprehensive shift briefs ensured no loss of continuity during shift changes

- An outstanding troubleshooter, she resolved more than 150 Network Control Center trouble tickets per month, more than any other tech, and reduced customer wait by 50%!

- As a volunteer bugler, in addition to his regular duties, he performed taps at 250 standard honors funerals including three ceremonies for active duty members.

- As a crew member, he contributed to the safe and efficient loading, transport, and set-up of heavy equipment valued at $300K and was responsible for the safe operation of trucks during deliveries.

- As a direct result of his exhaustive effort and preparation, the battalion earned two Mission Capable ratings during two CG inspections.

- As a network technician, he was responsible for the proper functioning and security of 30 NMCI workstations and successfully resolved 65 unique NMCI Help Desk tickets, providing expert assistance to users with challenging computer tasks and software problems.

- As a recruiter, he personally introduced numerous highly valuable members to the Naval service.

- As a repairer technician, completed 555 maintenance actions on 250 avionics components driving a turn-around rate that rivaled the much better staffed Nimitz.

- As a team member of the USNS Yukon food service crew, he contributed directly to their selection as recipient of the Captain David M. Cook Food Service Excellence Award.

- As Fire Controlman, Second Fleet, and "A" school detailer for E-5 and junior sailors, FC1 Smith's attention to detail was evident in 1,500 sets of orders and 125 Personnel Action Requests while maintaining a budget of $2 million annually.

- As GBS operator, she directed over 40 hours of fault isolation and circuit restoration for critical C4 networks. Her years of experience streamlined troubleshooting procedures and reduced average circuit restoral time by 50%.

- As Information Assurance Manager, IT1 Jones reviewed IA violations and implemented aggressive training to correct and train 150 joint personnel in IA security compliance. His efforts reduced security lapses by 50% while providing 100% IA Vulnerability Alert compliance for the first time in three years!

- As Senior Preventive Medicine Technician with MWSS 374, she conducted over 1,000 inspection across the

USCENTCOM AOR, including sanitary inspections of dining facilities, heads, berthing, and showers at Camp Dwyer.

- As submarine expediter, his proactive attention to detail resulted in 100% on-time completion of submarine availabilities with zero material delays.

- As the air conditioning and refrigeration manager, he contributed to maintaining the health and comfort of the entire crew, a key requirement for mission success.

- As training manager, he obtained three scarce regional AGS training slots, preventing delays in personnel qualification, and ensuring a qualified section before pending departure.

- As unit electromagnetic radiation safety officer, he scheduled initial and recurring inspections which ensured safe and reliable transmitter operations and interoperability with all other deck systems and prevented personnel injury and signal interference.

- Assisted Air Force personnel with developing their own calibration capability for their AN/ALC-99 Frequency Counter and transferred calibration responsibility for 11 units to the Air Force which saved 200 Navy man hours annually.

- Assisted in the delivery of over 200K gallons of JP-5 in support of five temporarily assigned CH-53 Sea Stallions which enabled the launch and rescue of American hostages.

- Assisted in development of procedures and certification processes for the new LPD-17 class ship, ensuring the new technology was safely and efficiently integrated into amphibious operations.

- Assisted in the installation of fiber optic network supporting Operation Deployed Data. Provided SEAL contingent with complete and rapid access to Air Tasking Order data and increased force readiness posture.

- Assisted in the redesign of our traditional tool system. Teamwork and initiative was rewarded with service-wide recognition for innovation and knowledge.

- Assisted shipmate in relocating his family to Sigonella Air Station, obtained room and board, helped with travel, work, and school arrangements to make transition as smooth as possible. His exceptional efforts set the standard which future moves will be compared to and ensured this new family will become a productive member of our Navy family.

- Brainstormed intelligence and technology integration efforts for several new platforms including unmanned vehicles.

- Briefed over 1,000 deploying marines pier-side on destinations and expected conditions. His proactive efforts increased unit effectiveness on arrival.

- Briefed several theater commanders and dignitaries on time-sensitive intelligence during operation. Her accurate and understandable reports enabled a cohesive and focused effort and ultimately, mission success.

- Building custodian for $12M passenger terminal, presented travelers with excellent first impression of Navy Air Mobility Command

- Built 100% accurate workstations and server databases for local system training exercises, LIGHTSABRE 07 and

COMBINED WARRIOR 09 and was directly responsible for zero failures!

- Calibrated more than 30 high-use, critical maintenance equipment tools and was directly responsible for the department's improved accuracy and performance

- Calibrated Cruise Missile Warhead Test Set needed to verify Tomahawk missile operation and reliability using new, locally-developed method which allowed more frequent testing and promoted confidence in operational readiness

- Chief Smith served as Ordnance Flight Deck Supervisor on the USS Bainbridge, loading over 50,000 lbs of live ordnance with a sortie completion rate of over 99.5%.

- Collected, exploited, and disseminated National Technical Means imagery in support of unit's Intelligence, Surveillance, and Reconnaissance (ISR) plan and intelligence reach-back operations, multiplying HQ situational awareness

- Committed to total quality: developed an innovative system for identifying, tracking, and correcting cockpit security discrepancies resulting in reduced aircraft down time due to cockpit FOD inspections

- Compiled detailed after-action reports which shaped future deployment strategies throughout the entire Joint Forces Command

- Completed scheduled modification of ship USC-38 antenna systems in less than half the allotted time

- Conducted 12 indoor air quality surveys which monitored 7 toxic gases ensuring closed environments were free from health hazards and capable of peak operations tempo.

- Conducted daily heat stress evaluations, protecting over 3,000 seaman and civilians across three piers

- Conducted numerous interior/exterior sweeps of Pax terminal during latest exercise, ensured terminal security and operational readiness

- Connected remote users to Navy Information Operations Command Maryland via Secure Internet Protocol Network, enhancing deployed JTF's operational capability

- Constructed bulletin board displays which provided 13,000 annual patients with preventive eyecare information

- Contributed 40 off-duty hours to environmental data migration; reviewed and brought 10 HAZMAT shop folders into compliance; exceeded COMSUBLANT goal by 20%

- Coordinated 22 priority unscheduled calibrations. Her actions remedied other agency failures and guaranteed USS Bainbridge deployment with full weapons complement

- Coordinated ground operations for Exercise SAFARI 2008 supporting Nigerian Military and Admiral Crunch resulting in a flawless, textbook operation

- Coordinated the safe movement of over 12,000 civilian passengers with the Deployment Control Center (DCC) and Base Operations

- Corrected several contractor-provided Software Installation Plans after an in-depth review. His attention to detail prevented a critical failure during underway operations.

- Created a communications status board for the SPINTCOM area which improved visibility and facilitated the tracking of circuit outages, projects, and other critical events

- Created a database that efficiently tracked ventilation equipment status in two dozen facilities. His regular review identified problem equipment and resulted in upgrades that improved air quality and production rates.

- Created an unprecedented plan that provided for Navy Reserve medical support for Homeland Defense dramatically improving the state's response to emergencies

- Decisive and reliable troubleshooting ability is directly responsible for squadron's expeditious repair rate and reduced aircraft downtime

- Dedicated to excellence, he orchestrated the relocation of the clinic's equipment which reduced patient travel and increased face-to-face time spent with providers by 20 percent

- Defended the department during two unexpected disbursing audits by Defense Accounting Office with his thorough knowledge with outstanding results.

- Delivered almost 200Mb of secure and reliable bandwidth to ships, subs, aircraft, and deployed troops.

- Demonstrated exceptional drive and leadership; his expert development of a junior division resulted in their stellar performance through an engineered refueling overhaul and two complex sea trial evolutions.

- Dependable seaman; he regularly disbursed and deposited over $20K of Norfolk Air Passenger Terminal's funds with 100% accountability.

- Deployed as primary C2IPS/CTAPS system administrator for Exercise AMAN 2008. Established CTAPS network in CVIC in record time, providing excellent mission support

- Deployed to NAS Sigonella, Italy, as our most experienced tech, during NAF Lajes runway closure and ensured a smooth transition of support

- Designed training program that improved the skills of subordinate observation teams and resulted in a 33% increase in capabilities during operations

- Detail oriented! Ship Commander packages and manifests were always available, accurate, and timely.

- Detained military members for DWI and identified two concealed weapons; disarmed and ensured the safety of all on-scene patrolmen and civilians

- Developed and implemented a weekly training review module in support of Joint Commission Readiness which focused effort and noticeable improved section performance

- Developed a new research methodology that improved the accuracy and timeliness of reports by 25%

- Developed and conducted imagery training for over three fourths of workcenter members. Produced the highest ratio of shift qualified personnel ever!

- Developed and tested NATO Integrated C2 software and identified many compatibility issues and provided solutions.

Her actions reduced unauthorized security accesses and provided an improved C2 infrastructure ahead of schedule.

- Devoted over 100 off-duty hours to the completion of administrative tasks, to include evaluations, correspondence, training, and management of 10 cross-assigned sailors

- Devoted to mission accomplishment. Volunteered to serve as squad leader for a 6 man security team providing force protection for base and surrounding housing areas

- Diligent material validation efforts led to the recovery of over $1,000,000 in AVDLR assets previously considered lost or destroyed

- Discovered unobserved P-3 cell pinhole leak; applied patch and eliminated depot-level repair requirement and $10K in repair cycle costs

- Disseminated daily image reports and indexes via SIPRNET: always 100% accurate, correctly formatted, and ahead of schedule

- During deployment, he assisted in the coordination and setup of 12 Tactical Operations Centers for 11 provincial reconstruction teams resulting in over 100 successful training evolutions.

- During INSURV 2010, his maintenance, in concert with each division's Damage Control Petty Officers, of the Operations Department's 5 work centers and 150 departmental spaces exceeded all expectations.

- During the Bainbridge inventory, he ensured that more than a hundred thousand dollars worth of vital equipment was properly stowed, accessible, and ready for use.

- Electronically mapped over 200 water main valves and updated USS Bainbridge database. Dedication and foresight ensured quick identification of failures and rapid restoral during emergency

- Enabled network monitoring within the AOR which expanded workcenter diagnostic capabilities and reduced dependency on outside agencies

- Established critical satellite link with NCTAMS during Exercise Joint Warrior; tested equipment, circuit, and carrier paths for reliability and provided error-free links which provided reliable communications for USS Anzio group and ensured operational success

- Evaluated NATO Integrated C2 software and identified compatibility issues between US and NATO systems which led to improved interoperability and prevented future comm failure

- Exceeded all expectation as fuel systems Chief during more than a dozen at-sea replenishments

- Excelled as Watch Officer, the only E-6 to be selected for this important E-7 position

- Exceptional shift leader. He led the shift in the detection of over 300 anomalies and 100 unscheduled area entries.

- Exhibited extensive job knowledge during exercise VALIANT SHIELD 09 and single-handedly solved numerous mission conflicts

- Exhibited quick decision making ability during Bahrain Crisis Response exercise scenarios. He executed post-attack

UXO sweeps and initiated Self Aid and Buddy Care for the injured.

- Expertly bore-sighted firing systems. Consistent aiming accuracy made live-target firing unnecessary and saved over 25K in ammo this fiscal year

- Expertly evaluated and prioritized over 260 job orders; developed short/long range goals for shop and accomplished an astounding 80% completion rate this quarter

- Expertly traced an arc fault on a submarine electrical distribution switchboard to a broken ground wire and saved over $30K on unnecessary contractor repairs

- Extensive technical knowledge and expert troubleshooting ability decreased equipment down time per quarter by 40%

- Facilitated the procurement of essential OR instrumentation which enabled Role 3 surgeons to provide critical life-saving surgeries

- Hazardous Material Awareness certified. Acquired skills needed to quickly identify hazardous incidents

- He aggressively coordinated over 20 subsistence deliveries valued at over 550k to more than 15 foreign ships improving our international relationships and expanding opportunities.

- He and his crew safely and professionally transferred more than 20 million gallons of POL products and over 5,000 pallets of stores and ordnance during a deployment that supported more than 120 replenishment events, numbers that far exceed deployment norms and the likes of which haven't been seen since the early days of OIF.

- He developed and formalized the Standard Operating Procedures for the new maintenance responsibility which justified $10M to be re-directed from non-viable projects to those capable of achieving technical and operational objectives.

- He developed and instructed over 100 seminars as a remediation tool for sailors struggling in high fail rate areas of all courses at ATT.

- He established the training course online using the Defense Department's Collaboration Web Tool, the first time IA training was available on-line, setting the stage for others to capitalize on his example.

- He prepared and organized 50 command instructions, policies, and designation letters, completing all the detachment's administrative requirements essential to logistics and mission readiness.

- He stood countless watches during the ship's qualification trials and underway evolutions to assure tests were conducted correctly.

- He supervised 13 Sailors in the medical support of the Camp Dwyer flightline construction project which produced the largest expeditionary airfield in Marine Corps history.

- He supervised over 100 deck evolutions during his two deployments including 25 UNREPs, 15 anchorings, and hundreds of helo and small boat operations, including VBSS and the Iraqi Arms, all finished with no safety incidents, a fleet first this FY.

- He trained and qualified 11 newly assigned personnel at several watch stations to improve watch stander efficiency and readiness.

- Helped stand up the Fleet Readiness Center which established capabilities and priorities that produced immediate movement toward goals

- Her attention to detail and dedication to readiness has increased the efficiency and productivity of the administrative department.

- Her deep involvement in our goals and unwavering dedication to duty was a force multiplier.

- Her meticulous inspections led the supply department to maintain 100% accountability of consumables and consolidated inventories and reduced the number of shipping containers required on site, cutting the recurring budget by 10%.

- His constant reviews and hard work as the bulk storage NCO significantly contributed to the success of the operation.

- His careful analysis of requirements, initiative, and determination increased battalion medical readiness from 50% to over 90% since his arrival 9 months ago.

- His diligent efforts in the processing of over 1,000 Availability Work Package components reduced the AWP turn-around time by 40%.

- His laborious preparation resulted in the Mental Health Directorate earning a 99% rating, the highest accreditation for 2009, setting a "benchmark of excellence" for others to strive for.

- His active training program and first-hand knowledge of the Purchase Card rules had tremendous impact on the supply department and was key to the department earning a grade of acceptable.

- His knowledgeable actions during Final Contract Trials (FCT) contributed significantly to the ship's early delivery and the highest FCT grade in T-AKE history.

- His implementation of WANX resulted in vastly increased network connectivity speed and a 50% productivity boost throughout the command.

- His skillful participation and oversight during 12 Joint Maritime Tactics Courses, 15 Group Commander training events, and 11 Fleet Synthetic Training exercises provided the highest quality training for hundreds of fleet officers and sailors and contributed substantially to fleet operational readiness.

- His technical acumen and forward thinking, continuously ensured that all circuit connections to the Global Information Grid were 100% reliable and secure.

- Identified and corrected three discrepancies in traffic handling/routing within his command's co-located sister unit restoring immediate command and control

- Identified overlooked broken pin on a S-3B main tank boost pump cannon plug. Expert troubleshooting saved more than $4,000 in unnecessary pump replacement

- Identified cracked UHF antenna base as the source of intermittent radio outages and repaired after more senior techs were unable to find problem. Restored communications and mission capability

- Identified critical error in image catalog references. His expert analysis and knowledge of system procedures prevented unnecessary missions and saved the strike group over $375K in fuel costs.

- Identified medical deployment deficiency trend and appointed 9 directorate immunization tracking system managers whose actions reduced medical deferrals by 50% and increased deployment readiness

- Identified the need for and developed the comprehensive AOR briefing which provided newly arriving members a road map to success and reduced attrition due to illness or injuries by 50%

- Implemented a proactive program to reduce tool shortages. Her new system saved over 400 man-hours and reduced shortages by 25% over a six month period.

- Implemented a web page for information dissemination which exponentially increased collaborative information sharing and greatly improved unit readiness

- Impressive tool control coordinator. He totally revised inventory procedures and, in less than thirty days, achieved zero discrepancies on the Quality Assurance audit.

- In addition to his already demanding duties and despite having no formal training, Petty Office Smith embraced the on-the-job-trainee position and devoted himself to providing the best medical service possible.

- In addition to his regular duties, he has, on his own initiative, become the resident expert and Program Manager for both of billeting's Ving and Identipass keycard systems.

- Increased support to COMSECONDFLT and Joint Forces Command Naval aviation by streamlining maintenance procedures and processes which reduced wait time for parts by 75%

- Initiated the transition of 400 personnel training records from paper files to a digital database, providing a more user friendly and efficient system.

- Instituted the coordination of multiple work crews via radio as dispatcher and reduced unnecessary trips by 30%

- Isolated chronic cross-talk noise problem on site's tactical interface panel to inadequate grounding and corrected a long-standing discrepancy which restored interface capabilities with tactical systems

- Key to his section's outstanding support for an emergency deployment to assess the damage of Wake Island after Typhoon Ioke struck. His support provided critical assistance to the USAF and directly enabled accurate casualty estimates within 48 hours

- Key to successful participation in JTFEX OPERATION BOLD STEP. Vigilant scrutiny of 100% of message traffic ensured quick reaction to changes and mitigated threats to the fleet

- Led aggressive electrical evaluation of carrier-wide HVAC systems and converted to local 220 VAC/50 hertz 30 days ahead of schedule

- Led the boiler manifold reseal team while the LCPO was deployed. She reduced fuel leaks and limited discrepancies to .25 per ship which exceeded the COMUSNAVCENT goal by 50% and set a new record

- Led the Strike Group in pollution prevention initiatives. Under his watch, the Bainbridge experienced a 25% reduction in long-term hazardous waste/material storage with no reduction in capability.

- Lost and Found representative. His continuous efforts resulted in the recovery of over 1200 lost bags and unparalleled customer service and satisfaction

- Made maximum use of pre-operational phase by acquiring new qualifications: completed the Senior Enlisted Propulsion Engineering Course (SEPEC), Fuel Testing, RODP, Fire fighting, and ADAMS for Supervisors

- Maintained 100% accountability of all COMSEC material under difficult circumstances

- Maintained an $18 million fixed asset property account with a 96.5% accuracy rating, the best rating in nine sections

- Maintained an amazing 100% fully mission-capable rate for entire FY 09 and shattered Second Fleet record of 99%!

- Maintained and directed the monthly logistics department inventories with no discrepancies despite a declining budget

- Maintained Land Mobile Radio system to the highest standard. His detailed management prevented interference and guaranteed critical communications at all times.

- Maintained over $200,000 in critical medical diagnostic and life-support equipment. His careful attention produced a 100% on-time calibration rate, ensured availability, and was vital to medical mission success!

- Maintenance expert: rebuilt aircraft intercom, a 2 hour fix accomplished in 30 minutes, enabling the delivery of 30 marines and 2 tons of relief supplies to remote Iraq province

- Managed Blood Alcohol Test program for SURFLANT units. His indisputable record of chain of custody and 100% accurate results was integral to shipmate morale, safety, and discipline.

- Managed more than 120 theater Promina nodes switching 120 GB of continuous bandwidth with 99.9% reliability!

- Managed the restoral of 3 of the most critical Pacific Network communication outages of 2009. Her decisive actions restored priority services and established protective measures which minimized the impact of future Pacific Network Operations failures.

- Managed the Electromagnetic Radiation Safety Program for the VFA-25 Fighter Squadron and ensured zero incidents of RF exposure and a safe work environment

- Medically supported over 1300 students during multiple high-risk training events. Volunteered to support Scout Swimmer, Water Survival, Naval Gunfire, and Inflatable Boat Operators Courses. His thorough hazard briefs, preparation, and readiness for any eventuality was directly responsible for zero injuries on his watch.

- Meticulously managed the CNE-CNA-C6F purchase card program and ensured that all purchases, valued in excess of $1M, were reconciled and certified with 100% accuracy.

- Modernized the section's outdated process for tracking safety and risk management issues. The logging rate is now at 100% for first time.

- Moved 20,000 passengers and 400 short tons of baggage with zero aircraft delays, a feat only possible due to an extremely proficient and well-trained team

- Networking guru who has connected all of Naval Station Great Lakes and is able to get the troops what they need without delay

- Orchestrated the relocation of the primary care clinic's diagnostic equipment with no interruption of service and reduced patient travel

- Organized a theater Intelligence team to exploit intelligence imagery collected by Pioneer UAV surveillance. His efforts doubled the section's capability and reduced JTF vulnerability.

- Organized and managed annual command-wide influenza inoculations for two medical commands. His focused yet flexible efforts produced a 100% inoculation rate in less than 3 weeks and made maximum use of finite vaccine resources with zero waste

- Organized, tracked, and embarked over 5,000 personnel from locations in the US, Kuwait, Iraq, Afghanistan, and other CENTCOM locations from point to point with 100% accountability

- Outstanding problem solver. Engineered a technical solution for SOCEUR reach-back communications requirements which provided a new communications capability, increased operational flexibility, and saved unknown thousands of dollars in development costs.

- Overcame all challenges while deployed in support of Operation DESERT STORM. He assisted in the short-notice relocation of the critical Air Operations Center to Eskan Village, Saudi Arabia. Their well-coordinated cutover limited data interruption to less than one hour!

- Oversaw the construction of $8.5M construction project at Mustang and became the first reserve battalion to exceed build-in-place time limits with the highest score to date despite being severely undermanned.

- Perfectly supported 1200 deployed seamen and ensured a safe operating environment that facilitated the achievement of all objectives

- Performed active, preventive maintenance and phase inspections on power distribution systems. His regular inspections resulted in zero mishaps and 100% reliability.

- Performed as observer/controller during five marine exercises and was integral to the overall success of Special Forces assessments

- Performed Collateral Damage Estimates and analysis of over 2,000 joint missions during Operation Enduring Freedom. She identified long-overlooked effects which resulted in modified mission procedures theater-wide.

- Performed complicated frequency converter and amplifier frequency response and gain alignments which enabled

100% operational redundancy and was directly responsible for the high satellite link reliability rate

- Performed emergency calibration of Spectrum Analyzer for NAS Point Mugu Airborne Command and Control squadron and saved an otherwise grounded mission

- Performed through end-of-deployment and phase inspections so detailed that they resulted in the least number of discrepancies in INSURV records ever

- Performed flawlessly during NEPTUNE WARRIOR training course. The skills gained increased interoperability among NATO coalition forces and facilitated flow of intel between allied ships.

- Performed over 200 S-3 Viking fuel system repairs. His diligent efforts enabled over 16K squadron flying hours!

- Performed an extensive program review on his own initiative which ultimately delivered a 100% pass rate on all 10 sectors during the formal scheduled inspection

- Performed pump tests at 11 stations ensuring optimum fleet readiness and contributed to an Excellent rating in the Nov 08 INSURV Inspection

- Performed QA sound analysis and vibration measurements for 12 submarines during overhaul and repair. Identified undocumented sound short that transmitted noise through the ship hull and arranged the modification to all similar class subs to maintain fleet superiority

- Performed System Admin duties on Theater Battle Management Core Systems (TBMCS) suite in support of Operation Enduring Freedom. Ensured 12 TBMCS servers,

70 client workstations, and 10 remote workstations provided continuous Air Tasking Order dissemination to all units

- Performed weekly preventive maintenance on the SPS-49 Very Long-Range Air Surveillance Radar resulting in a phenomenal zero failures in 12 months, the best rate in the Strike Group

- Petty Officer Smith developed Fire Control Air Warfare grade sheets for the MK-92 and close-in weapon systems for fleet-wide use which standardized procedures fleet wide.

- Petty Officer Smith diligently and successfully complied with all requirements for the 2010 Command Cyber Readiness Inspection, earning an outstanding score of 95.5.

- Petty Officer Smith exceeded expectations as a sailor embedded with an army unit, coordinating and executing complex missions that resulted in numerous lives saved from IEDs.

- Petty Officer Jones' relentless efforts and technical expertise played a vital role in the successful completion of the 20-week Aegis test program.

- Planned and implemented a direct internet connection for the C2IPS system at JTFSA in support of SOUTHERN WATCH which supplied a first-ever joint intelligence and planning capability

- Played a demanding and central role in exercises Key Resolve 2010 and Ulchi Freedom Guardian 2010 which optimized Command and Control of both the entire U.S. Pacific Command and U.S. Forces Korea.

- Prepared $27M vehicle fleet for the largest typhoon ever to hit Pearl Harbor. His preventive actions preserved the fleet as 100% operational.

- Prepared work center personnel for their qualification evaluations. Her intensive efforts increased the work center pass rate by 50% and now leads the DESRON.

- Processed 100% of customers inventories/schedules, delivering 255 products, the first time meeting all requirements this year

- Processed over 2500 patient records requests monthly with such care that, on inspection, all records complied 100% with HIPPA standards

- Processed thousands of NAVMACS messages at ship Communications Center under all conditions with an accuracy rate of over 99%

- Productive team member. His heroic efforts provided continuous mission support even while 30% of the department was deployed.

- Provided agile readiness support! Reviewed and prepared over 2K troops for deployment in less than 10 days. 100% met requirements and deployed on time.

- Provided convoy training to 34 Chief Petty Officers prior to short-notice deployment to USCENTCOM AOR and increased their readiness upon arrival

- Provided five star service to ship personnel

- Provided full range of on-demand cryptologic support and tailored SIGINT advice and assistance to high profile CJCS mission to meet high tempo demands

- Published revised civilian provider formulary. Enhanced 7,500 patients' and community's care and non-stocked requests dropped by 50%.

- Quick decision making during Bahrain Crisis Response exercise scenarios edged out competitors and won the All-AOR Readiness Challenge

- Quickly mastered all facets of the 7th Fleet's largest distribution element and increased section productivity by 25% within 3 months of arrival

- Quickly replaced a defective diesel-electric engine feed manifold valve while underway, installing the new component in only 5 hours, 2 hours ahead of schedule!

- Quickly qualified in all aspects of the Flight Operations department, he took the initiative to learn how to operate equipment or process requirements in peripheral stations including Fuels and CE Maintenance.

- Reacted quickly under pressure to reprogram the Mission Display Unit on the USS Coronado and restored a working interface and Tomahawk missile launch capability

- Rearranged the entire squadron's tool control program and raised daily accountability to 100%

- Rebuilt intercom cord/microphone switch on the spot; two hour fix accomplished in minutes; landed navy seal team in Iraq in time to liberate prisoners

- Received accolades from C5RA assessors for the superior performance of weapons, radar, and data systems.

- Received trans load training and is thoroughly qualified; decontaminated/stored pallets while in MOPP4, is ready for any combat eventuality!

- Recommended use of user-friendly thermostats and filter replacement media which modernized our facilities while reducing energy use

- Reconfigured 10 tactical satellite missions to conserve finite satellite resources and increased bandwidth available to ships by 15%

- Reduced delays in patient processing by building bulletin board instructions which improved service for 2,000 annual patients

- Reinvented customer service. From user-choice menus to seating arrangements and hours, totally revised culinary service; recognized by the Commander

- Repaired faults in the helm, IFF, and SPS-64 systems ensuring 100% reliability during multi-national exercise Joint Warrior

- Repaired a Fuel Quantity Test Set for the NAVAIR Lakehurst maintenance unit. His on-site fix saved the Navy 3K in parts and ensured uninterrupted fuel support.

- Replaced number 4 main tank compensator probe under hazardous conditions. Her heroic efforts restored the engine and preserved the safety of ship and personnel.

- Reprogrammed the USS Nimitz bridge digital systems control computer negating the need for contractor repair and saving over $60K in repair costs

- Resolved SH-2 Seasprite fuel low level indication during critical exercise. Adjusted the in-tank level sensor to insure accurate fuel quantity readings, cleared aircraft for immediate launch and successful exercise completion.

- Resourceful. Obtained two scarce Remote Mine Hunting System training slots and increased Minesweeper personnel qualifications to 90%

- Responded to emergency Class 3 fuel spill and stopped the leak and contained the contaminant in less than 5 minutes, minimizing the effect on the environment

- Responded to suspicious package report and assisted NCIS in recovering suspicious contents. His quick action prevented hazard to team and onlookers.

- Restored over 600 communications circuit/link outages as they occurred across the Pacific theater keeping comm link availability rate above 99.99%, an unparalleled uptime!

- Reviewed, updated, corrected five key Software Installation Plans. His proactive oversight prevented critical Command and Control delay.

- Revised and updated all workcenter continuity books, a key factor in the excellent rating earned during Pacific Fleet inspection 2008

- Revived the flagging hearing protection program. Conducted noise studies in over a dozen shops and implemented preventive measures that reduced potential hearing loss by an estimated 50%

- Scheduled both recurring and emergency maintenance on work center equipment ensuring data on target at 99% rate!

- Scheduled course dates for officer and enlisted military members to attend and made maximum use of available slots

- Served as the Government Purchase Card agency program coordinator managing three approving officials and eleven cardholders across three commands

- Served as witness for NCIS and Legal Office in UCMJ actions and provided bullet-proof documentation to ensure Navy standards were upheld

- Set up forms and publications accounts for six branches and was integral to DESRON operations!

- She completed over 500 reports, improving the overall MARADMIN compliance from a low 25% to over 90%, the highest in the III MEF and island-wide.

- She worked overtime trouble-shooting issues in software upgrades to all 90 workstations, ensuring command-wide workstation readiness and reliability.

- Skillful administrator and manager committed to total quality. Responsible for changes in Quality Assurance audit program that streamlined the audit process and enhanced mission effectiveness.

- Skillfully supervised the detailed electronic tuning of the ship's periscope and ESM systems prior to its first overseas deployment. His efforts resulted in zero faults and optimum performance throughout the deployment.

- Solved numerous problems with remote terminals. He traced connection failures like a pro!

- Sound judgment ensured the successful conversion of medical personnel records to the Defense Medical Human Resources System and IAA program. Improved data accuracy and reduced delays in personnel assignments during the last five contingency operations by 50%

- Spearheaded over 70 STEP assignments supporting satellite reach back for RIMPAC 08, the world's largest international maritime exercise

- Spotted and stopped taxiing C-130 from colliding with fire bottle. His alert vigilance and quick action prevented the loss of aircraft and equipment.

- Stellar up-keep of $5,000,000 vehicle fleet achieved a 99% in-commission rate, the best readiness rates in memory

- Streamlined patient in-processing procedures and increased patient face-to-face time spent with medical providers by 25%

- Superb manager. Programmed/executed recurring work orders with an impressive 100% completion rate

- Supercharged the radiation safety program. Her thorough review of all workcenters ensured 100% Nuclear Regulatory Commission compliance.

- SUPERIOR PERFORMER! Excelled during JTF Exercise Operation BOLD STEP. His meticulous equipment checks identified comm failure before operations start and repaired.

- Superior performer! Integral to the delivery of over 30M gallons of DFM fuel to more than 1,000 ships annually. He responded to over 1200 servicings and maintained an impressive 15-minute average response time.

- Superior performer! Certified over 60 items of TMDE and was key to the laboratory's 5 day backlog, the lowest backlog in 5 years

- SUPERIOR TECHNICIAN. Independent of outside assistance, he identified and repaired over 22 major mission degrading casualties to the AN/SQQ-32 SONAR, always ensuring a fully functional sonar.

- Supervised the implementation of both DMS and Navy SCI LCC aboard the Nimitz. His actions secured a smooth transition from the legacy message system.

- Supervised the repair of air conditioning at Naval Network Warfare Command facilities and rescued $3M of critical communications equipment from imminent destruction

- Supported the Command with over 50 in-office sick call hours and over 670 field sick call hours. Changed office hours in response to needs, improved service availability to ship personnel, increased number of personnel seen by 20%

- TECHNICAL ABILITY! Displayed decisive management skills during TERMINAL FURY. Engineered constantly changing theater comm networks for ships chopping in and out of the AOR with zero delays to real-world missions

- The first-ever enlisted procurement specialist, he became level 1 qualified 3 months ahead of schedule and developed procedures for and processed contracts valued at over 200k.

- The purpose of her tireless efforts became evident through three consecutive maritime exercises that were conducted safely and mishap free.

- Tireless achiever. He maintained a 100% on-time departure rate during Joint Exercise Noble Anvil

- Traced chronic problem on faulty alarm interface panel to open resistor and replaced restoring a critical monitoring capability

- Traced intermittent UHF and VHF radio system outages to a grounded headset and prevented a critical mission scrub

- Traced long-standing problem between Military Sealift Command system and TBMCS to an existing improper configuration. The correction improved data transfer rate and saved over 500 man hours per month.

- Trained 12 newly assigned personnel on crisis response procedures and significantly enhanced war-fighting abilities

- Trained new personnel on Document Exploitation (DOCEX) team in the Multinational Division-Southern Area of Operations. All members shift-qualified ahead of schedule, increased the AO's exploitation potential by 50%

- Trained and established roles for six Battlestaff watch officers in preparation for USEUCOM's largest exercise, DARK ANVIL 08. Provided successful operational direction supporting over 20K troops

- Troubleshot failure of a 688 class submarine AN/APX-72 receiver/transmitter and repaired in less than 10 minutes, resumed scheduled operations with no delays

- Troubleshot loss of SIPRNET connectivity, isolated to failed router and rerouted, restored high priority data

- Troubleshot over 350 PC and circuit outages to resolution; professional support to ship personnel

- Updated and purged message pickup and release folder; reduced redundant efforts and increased focus on supported commands' personnel rosters

- Updated Navy TCAIMS program for all deploying personnel with 100% accuracy. Attention to detail directly and positively affected morale and readiness.

- Using his knowledge and experience he accomplished two depot-level repairs in theater and saved the Navy over $80k and returned both aircraft to FMC status, restoring mission readiness.

- Utilized existing equipment and spare parts to assemble needed test rack. Improved functionality and saved work center $3K in material costs

- Utilized process improvement techniques to reduce military performance reporting delays by 55%

- Validated/scrubbed 68 PMEL accounts. Overcame the loss of records due to personnel rotations and restored vital oversight

- Volunteered to augment NAS Norfolk ramp services during peak hours. Loaded 747 cargo during hottest summer on record. Great team player!

- Volunteered to load baggage and operate step truck for POTUS entourage. His performance showcased Military Sealift Command professionalism.

- Volunteered to perform visual tests at local elementary school; promoted health of over 250 community students

- Volunteered to serve as Naval Gunfire Liaison Officer, an O2 duty, and provided failsafe coordination between Fire Control Party and multiple firing platforms. He ensured personnel and equipment safety while raising targeting accuracy to record levels.

- Was instrumental in the development of a core group of watch standers for the Regional Operations Center, providing vital continuity to a mission critical watch

- With the CRSP team he inspected over 400 sea bags, 225 footlockers, 2700 weapons, 2200 tri-walls and inspected more than 225,000 total items.

- Worked extensively with C4I Department on several complex interdepartmental equipment networking faults, utilizing his experience to solve them quickly with minimal resultant impact on combat readiness.

- Worked hand-in-hand with joint-service multi-national coalition forces. Overcame communication barriers and safely delivered 250K gallons of DFM fuel to Korean contingent

- Worked tirelessly to prepare for INSURV inspection and is directly responsible for strong rating earned

- Worked to realign ESAMS with directorate structure, providing accurate and useful reporting information

Climate/Equal Opportunity

- Active and perceptive, kept chain of command apprised of racial and sexual climate conditions and prevented obstacles to ship harmony

- Administered two surveys to personnel to assess command climate. Identified areas of concern and submitted improvement recommendations.

- Advocated for an anti-discrimination work environment that paid big dividends in morale, loyalty, and productivity

- As a member of the Command Assessment Team, he helped to improve the perception of equal opportunity throughout the Command.

- As Command Career Counselor, the entire crew depends on and benefits from his guidance.

- As Command Equal Opportunity Officer, his example and leadership cultivated an atmosphere of understanding, harmony, and esprit de corps throughout the command.

- As Command Equal Opportunity Officer, his effective training and unwavering principles were directly responsible for command climate improvement as measured by an exemplary annual assessment.

- Chief Jones is a staunch advocate of tradition, loyalty, and strong Naval service. His unwavering support of the chain of command, firm enforcement of military standards, and equitable treatment of subordinates has optimized morale and promoted teamwork and mission accomplishment.

- Communicated duty effects on section climate, led to plans for improvement, increased satisfaction and morale

- CS2 Smith has been a vital asset as a member of the Command assessment team where she helped to improve the overall equal opportunity atmosphere throughout the command.

- Deckplate leadership produced the most professional mixed-gender working environment I've ever seen; zero sexual harassment issues!

- DEDICATED TO NAVY's CORE VALUES. Ensured that all Sailors are challenged with opportunities to excel within the workcenter, thereby increasing in-rate satisfaction and ultimately, retention

- Directly responsible for extremely low disciplinary rate in the line division. Genuinely concerned with subordinate's personal and professional growth

- Elevated several unobserved yet critical issues that threatened the unity of our department which defused an explosive work environment and improved production

- Encouraged camaraderie by example which opened avenues for discussion and trust

- Fostered an atmosphere of understanding, trust, and tolerance; increased team effort shattered all records!

- Identified areas of concern and submitted improvement recommendations

- Impeccable demeanor and role model. He is the true image of Navy Core Values. He taught and practiced exemplary Equal Opportunity and contributed to the high morale of the crew.

- Organized and oversaw ship's Asian American celebration; promoted knowledge and understanding of racial diversity

- Proactive specialist in equal opportunity and diversity. Admired for high standards and fair treatment.

- Relayed department's deep concerns to chain of command, spiked morale

- Reported aboard as Chief of the Boat and immediately improved the crew's morale and performance. A genuine leader, he has an innate ability to facilitate teamwork and motivate his peers and subordinates to achieve ship's goals.

- Role Model. Positively impacted Command by establishing professional and productive work climate and successfully completing all Pre-commissioning Unit Instructions.

- Selected as COMMAND NEO Coordinator; managed most critical program with utmost care and efficiency

- Selected by commander for his subtle yet effective leadership style to head up Organizational Climate program

- Serves as Command Sexual Assault Victim Intervention (SAVI) Coordinator, a critical service that maintains morale

- STANDOUT MENTOR! An active, dedicated CMEO, led by example and encouraged equal treatment and opportunity for all Navy members. Climate assessment results demonstrated improved morale and increased understanding of and support for Navy policies.

- Strengthened command climate and morale by promoting good order and discipline. Ensured exceptional crew conduct during two foreign port visits which promoted favorable international relations

- Superior leadership skills fostered most united team on ship; workcenter had least reported EO incidents in fleet

- Took steps to protect sensitive information from disclosure, preventing unnecessary embarrassment and maintaining an atmosphere of trust and cooperation.

- United a team of active duty and reserve seamen into one cohesive and productive organization.

- Volunteered to serve as Navy Equal Opportunity/Sexual Harassment (NEOSH) survey coordinator, empathetic methods enhanced accuracy, opened avenue to increased integration, promised success as unit

Military Bearing and Character

The category of Military Bearing and Character includes comments on behavior concerning appearance, conduct on and off-duty, physical fitness, character, and adherence to the Navy's core values. Examples of comments that address these characteristics follow.

- Accelerated professional growth by serving hundreds of hours as Flight Line Coordinator, a billet normally filled by a Chief Petty Officer

- As Honor Guard for NOSC St. Louis, BM3 Smith upheld the Navy's greatest tradition of service by honoring those that served before him.

- CAPABLE PROFESSIONAL. Was selected to act as Anti-Air Warfare Commander during joint exercise NEPTUNE WARRIOR. His stalwart efforts improved communications with other members of Strike Group and resulted in 100% identification and immediate response to threat.

- CE2 Gonzalez leads by example. He inspires others with his professional military bearing, exceptional work quality and quantity, and his consistent positive attitude.

- Consistently achieves the highest standard of excellence and displays pride in work

- Coordinated and participated in a traditional training event onboard the USS BAINBRIDGE similar to the CPO inductee program aboard the USS MISSOURI. Participation demonstrated care and concern for subordinates and helped ensure Navy traditions and pride endure

- Crisp uniforms, razor-sharp military bearing

- Devoted many hours of off-duty time to ensure unit's training requirements were met. All department trainees were fully qualified in minimum time which dramatically improved the section's effectiveness.

- Displayed exceptional pride in personal image. He wears immaculate, inspection-ready uniforms at all times.

- Effective Communicator and Manager: PO1 Smith rarely requires oversight; always provides efficient, timely reporting and trend metrics for unit physical readiness, medical, and training requirements.

- Exceptional CPO. His superb military image made him the obvious selection for NCOIC of the unit Honor Guard.

- Exemplary management skill and organizational foresight. He personifies command allegiance, military bearing, and a strong code of ethics.

- Exemplifies the highest standards of moral integrity and personal honor. Capable and dedicated, he demonstrated extraordinary discipline.

- Hand-picked to instruct 50 students in advanced Installation Defense skills at the Joint Readiness Training Center

- He provided continuous motivation through leadership and is an effective communicator and a model Sailor and manager to shipmates and subordinates.

- Helped renovate the USS Constitution CPO living spaces for the CPO Selectee Legacy Academy

- Highly Dedicated to the Navy. Selflessly volunteered for a nine month IA, certified early as CTF72 Task Force Watch Supervisor and, despite a demanding schedule, has began his graduate studies.

- His willingness to accept new and challenging duties is a testimony to his character and is in keeping with the Navy's core values of honor, courage, and commitment.

- Inexhaustible commitment and determination. He provided sound leadership to 40 Sailors, 15 civilians and 10 junior officers, while providing quality support services to 10 medical service providers.

- Led by example: conducted biweekly PT sessions for 5 departments and increased fitness across the board

- Mature supervisor with the confidence to accept criticism while retaining the ability to trust his own judgment

- MENTOR AND LEADER. As Senior Enlisted Leader, he solved many housing, medical, and personnel issues. The cornerstone of our team, taking care of our Sailors is his top concern.

- NON-STOP SELF-IMPROVEMENT. Completed the USAF NCO Academy in-residence course. Completed 3 credit hours (Sociology) toward AA.

- Organized the 2008 Hawaii Navy Ball, a hallmark event for over 1000 sailors and their families; reinforced pride in service and commitment by families to the Navy way of life.

- Outstanding role model. His embodiment of Navy core values guarantees success. Promoted naval tradition and pride as Master of Ceremonies for two poignant retirement ceremonies.

- Peerless uniform and appearance; adheres to NAVPERS 15665I at all times and sets the example for peers and subordinates

- Petty Officer Smith has continued to be a key player in providing continued leadership essential to mission accomplishment.

- PO Gonzalez developed and maintained an intensive physical fitness program that improved morale and reduced the semi-annual failure rate by over 50%!

- Provided an excellent role model for subordinates through individual actions and resilient character. Scored OUTSTANDING on PRT.

- Razor sharp military bearing. Consistently scored grades of outstanding on the command's semiannual PRT

- Ready to deploy on short notice, to meet any contingency, anywhere in the world

- Selected as top performer of the month for May, 2007; displayed exemplary leadership and professionalism

- Selected for advancement to E-6 under the Command Advancement Program

- Standards and professional competence generated immediate confidence and improved subordinate morale

- Superior military image led to selection as the USN representative during the SPAWAR tree lighting ceremony

- Supported new USS CONSTITUTION-like CPO inductee event aboard USS MISSOURI; promoted pride in service

- Takes exceptional pride in personal appearance and presents a meticulous military image

- Top Seaman! Selected as CGC BELUGA's Sailor of the Quarter for the second quarter 2008

- Wears immaculate inspection-ready uniform on a daily basis with a positive attitude and outlook

Teamwork

- A dynamic Senior Enlisted Advisor (SEA), he increased communication between the ranks and increased overall satisfaction at work.

- A True Team Player. Flawlessly prepared and executed the administration required for an operation vital to national security and a 6-month Western Pacific Deployment

- Aided Facility Management for 3 months, while maintaining his own demanding duties, showing great efficiency and enthusiasm when tasked

- As Command CFL, his tireless efforts strengthened the culture of fitness onboard resulting in zero PRT failures and removing 10 sailors from FEP status.

- As directorate Leading Petty Officer, he seamlessly assumed duties as acting LCPO and Assistant Department head during a crucial gap in the CPO billet.

- Assisted the squadron in receiving an adjective grade of OUTSTANDING during the COMNAVAIRLANT HAZMAT inspection

- By consistent cross-training of ET and Quartermaster personnel, he developed a versatile and effective Navigation Team which naturally and gradually eliminated interagency rivalry and increased productivity of both departments.

- Continually assisted Line Division during off-duty hours by training and qualifying personnel for shift duty

- Cross-trained into the Material Control shop to assist the division during a manpower shortage; ensured all workcenters received their parts and materials promptly

- Dedicated to team success; volunteered for additional duties which included coaching and instructing.

- Demonstrating an in-depth knowledge of his rating, Petty Officer Smith accepted extra responsibilities as the Force Protection and Electronic Warfare Subject Matter Expert which reduced travel, costs, and man-power for two different warfare areas.

- Directly contributed to the USS Bainbridge receiving the Battle "E" and Arleigh Burke Award

- During manning shortages, Petty Officer Smith acted as the sole primary provider to 525 Marines and Sailors, ensuring uninterrupted Primary Care service to the entire battalion.

- ENTHUSIASTIC TRAINER! Ensured sailors rotated positions during normal cruising watches to provide broadest possible experience. Inclusive efforts increased crew qualification, confidence, and teamwork.

- Extremely diversified. Sought out new ways to aid in Command enhancement and Sailorization by organizing public outreach opportunities and volunteering hundreds of hours in support of Joint Color guard events, NRC fundraising, and local elementary schools.

- Gifted motivator. Led his team in reducing "awaiting maintenance" discrepancies to 98% and drastically reduced "repeat discrepancies"

- He dutifully executed his responsibilities as President of the Enlisted Association leading 44 Sailors to complete 3 fund raisers which raised $2200 and contributed $900 to the 2010 Hospital Corpsman Ball.

- Helped reorganize section into an efficient, streamlined shop and reduced late reports for all training requirements to zero

- Major contributor to the Department's high state of readiness which was certified by an impressive 98% sortie completion rate

- Motivational Skills: effectively ran the unit's Operations Division. PO1 Smith inspires esprit de corps and teamwork through his lead by example style of leadership.

- Motivated team player: contributed off duty time and effort to support unit and community activities

- On return from an extended one year deployment, Petty Officer Smith shared knowledge gained with unit personnel leading to all members being more prepared, emotionally and operationally, for their scheduled deployments.

- Participated in Airman Leadership School renovation; improved quality of life for over 2,200 joint students

- Petty Officer Jones constantly invigorates subordinates to perform all missions to the absolute limit of their abilities. Top achiever with boundless potential.

- Petty Officer Smith's law enforcement expertise and experience proved invaluable in integrating the unit with the existing active duty Security Force.

- Serving as Administrative Petty Office, she aided in the advancement of many newly reporting personnel by preparing special evaluations and identifying missing award points or evaluations.

- Skill and initiative are balanced by his genuine concern for peers and subordinates.

- Strong community involvement. Supports CFC and Navy Relief. Volunteers off-duty time for Wildlife Response Rescue and Rehabilitation Group

- Team Builder. Instills professionalism and cooperation. Displayed superior leadership while performing NAV/OPS LCPO duties

- Team player with initiative. Provided invaluable assistance to central technical publications librarian resulting in zero discrepancies during a recent inspection

- Team player. Active participant in both VA-34 and USS George Washington (CVN 73) First Class Association

- Team player. Actively involved in squadron's recent successful Conventional Weapons Technical Proficiency Inspection

- Team player. Through his outstanding personal example, provided necessary guidance and supervision to ensure all tasks were successfully completed.

- Total team player. Intimately involved in the planning and execution of numerous successful fund raising projects for the First Class Association.

- Trained 4 SCO successors in half the usual time required; increased shift expertise 75%.

- Unselfish team player. Spent numerous off-duty hours ensuring five Petty Officers attained their Low/High Power Engine Turn-up qualification

- Versatile Team-player. Makes his technical expertise a squadron-wide asset. Eagerly volunteers to assist any workcenter with any task.

- Volunteered for and served as Command Equal Opportunity Officer and Command Ozone Depletion Officer

- Volunteered for Commander's change of command ceremony; excellent military community involvement

- Volunteered to serve as NEOSH representative and presented seven topical briefings at All Hands

- When the clinic needed someone to work in the pharmacy, HM2 Smith answered the call and assumed the role, sparing his section from losing qualified members.

- With his team player attitude, he became a force multiplier allowing the Pearl Harbor Naval Shipyard admin office to become self-reliant and 100% mission-capable even with up to a 50% reduction of staff.

Leadership

- A dynamic Senior Enlisted Advisor, he bridged the gap between the ranks and increased overall satisfaction at work.

- A moral leader, committed to providing the best quality of life and training for Sailors

- A respected leader, he sets and expects stringent, yet achievable, performance standards for subordinates.

- A self-starter, he completes many tasks before others realize that they need to be done.

- Active involvement reduced PRT failures to 10 percent for the first time in two years.

- Agile technical ability and foresight was directly responsible for successful transition from traditional three-level maintenance to evolving two-level standard.

- Always putting his Sailors' success at the forefront, he exemplifies true deckplate leadership.

- An example to his peers and subordinates. Always placed mission first and has an unquestionable devotion to duty

- As a member of the MWR Heritage Committee and the Coalition of Sailors Against Destructive Decisions, she played an active role in encouraging smart decisions by military members.

- As BEQ Liaison, his sound and logical leadership brought the barracks into compliance with MED IG standards. He obtained approval for over $400k in upgrades which dramatically improved the residents' quality of life.

- As the Command Mentor Coordinator, he instituted a Mentorship Program which benefited 50 sailors and resulted in 100% retention, increased off-duty education, and improved morale and productivity.

- Assumed full oversight of the special warfare program; improved prospecting practices and mentorship of program candidates and achieved program goals ahead of schedule for all of FY10

- By consistent cross-training of personnel, he developed a versatile and effective Navigation Team which successfully piloted the ship through numerous unfamiliar ports under the worst visibility conditions ever encountered by this group.

- By personal example, he inspired his subordinates to strive for increasing levels of excellence and provided a motivational catalyst for their success.

- CM3 Smith's commitment to excellence led the way to success for Bravo Company and NMCB 21.

- CMD DAPA. Headed the base-wide alcohol de-glamorization campaign; through aggressive coordination with tenant commands and off-base businesses, his preventive efforts produced a 50% reduction in alcohol related incidents.

- Coached shipmates to win both ship and Group Junior Sailor of the Quarter Boards

- Competent Command Master Chief. As Acting CMC, he encouraged base-wide CPO involvement in CPO initiation ceremonies, revitalized the Sailor of the Quarter program, and increased retention by 25%.

- Consistently leads from the front during training scenarios

- Created a Mentorship Program and mentored 25 troops; achieved 100% retention and increased education by 50%. Chaired 20 CDBs to ensure the promotion of the best; reinstituted the Sailors Creed recital during quarters, embraced and bolstered tradition

- DECKPLATE LEADER. Intrusive leadership yielded one Sailor of the Quarter, 100% eligible advanced, 100% passed both PRT cycles, 100% enrolled in USMAP, and 50% college enrollments.

- Dedicated leader. Directly responsible for extremely low disciplinary rate in the line division. Genuinely concerned with subordinate's personal and professional growth

- Demanded the best training environment for Sailors and accepted nothing less than total participation and quality results

- Developed a cross-training program and self-directed work atmosphere that improved watch member productivity by 90%

- Developed a Joint Mentorship Program that facilitated a climate of kinship throughout the command providing guidance to over 120 joint personnel and resulting in 90% retention

- Developed Sailors through positive counseling, coaching, and mentoring. Instilled a mission-first attitude; motivated entire unit to do the same.

- Directed unit and active duty Navy personnel as team leader during UNITAS deployment greatly improving contingency knowledge; surpassed all expectations; hands-on leadership was the catalyst for the entire effort.

- Directly and positively impacted the performance and careers of 75 personnel as the Mentorship Coordinator. Took over a failing program and revitalized it, increasing participation by 80% and retention by 25%.

- Displayed a genuine concern for Sailors. Motivated his crew to perform to the best of their ability as individuals and as a unit.

- Distinguished herself from her peers with her initiative and unmatched technical expertise while continuing to learn from others

- EFFECTIVE TRAINER! Ensured Sailors rotated positions during normal cruising watches to provide broadest possible experience which increased crew qualification and capability

- Effectively led and inspired sub-standard sailors to willingly improve and perform to Navy standards

- Enforced military standards and chain of command for Navy and sister services; increased members' pride in service

- Enrolled every member of his workcenter in the CLEP Program to earn college credit

- Excellent Mentor. Personal drive and ambition helped produce five in-rate advancements. Worked with Sailors to assist them in overcoming shortfalls in training and performance and provided guidance on outside resources when needed

- EXPERIENCED LEADERSHIP. Management and supervisory skills command maximum performance and ensure combat readiness. Dynamic leadership of his Department throughout the ship's first Persian Gulf deployment, safely traversing 12,000 nautical miles, can be summed up in one word: Magnificent!

- Expertly led the actions inside the Damage Control Center (DCC) during the COMNAVSURFPAC IMX. His efforts were praised by the Nuclear Inspection Team inspectors.

- Expertly prepared his department for a Eastern Atlantic deployment. Ensured the NAV/OPS Department was always in excellent material condition and ready for sustained effective performance at sea.

- Firmly supports the squadron. Single-handedly resurrected a demoralized First Class association and established a "can do" spirit. Initiated numerous successful fund raising projects.

- Gifted leader. Directly responsible for turning around the production effectiveness of the airframes workcenter, resulting in grades of Outstanding on QA and COMATKWINGLANT audits.

- He distinguished himself as a respected and effective leader by his in-depth knowledge of Navy programs and professional guidance of junior personnel.

- He mentored all Sailors within the department, set the highest standards for customer service, and championed the crew's needs in all respects.

- He passed down knowledge and experience gained to junior Sailors, ensuring the proper training of the next generation of naval professionals.

- He revived and led the 1st Class Petty Officers' Association of over 100 Junior Officers, increasing morale and teamwork.

- Her steadfast commitment to her Sailors' personal and professional growth facilitated the recognition of one of her troops as Sailor of the Quarter and another as nominee for Yeoman of the Year.

- Her superb managerial skills pushed our clinic to win the TRICARE Regional Access Award for 2 consecutive years.

- His diligent and detailed management of the ship's store earned a grade of Excellent during the Logistic Management Assessment.

- His lead from the front approach consistently produced exceptional results; his division earned an unparalleled overall score of 98% during our 3M assessment.

- His leadership efforts, while at SOCEUR, have shown unparalleled success. Under his outstanding tutelage, three members were advanced to E-7 and four to E-6.

- His outstanding administration of the divisional 3-M program resulted in zero deficiencies during Type Commander 3-M inspections

- His tenacious attitude and commitment to putting group goals ahead of personal priorities was inspirational and motivated his peers to deliver the most accurate and capable system possible.

- Implemented a maintenance program that increased the Construction Battalion Unit's overall operational readiness rate from 50% to over 90% in only 6 months

- Implemented an internal random evaluation program for her workcenter that increased formal evaluation scores by 50% in just six weeks.

- Innovative administrator. Supported 9 active aviation maintenance activities and 3 detachments with all required tools and parts. His increased interaction with supported units increased focus on expected service and dramatically reduced delays and lowered the non-capable status to lowest level in 5 years.

- Inspirational Leader. He trained his junior yeomen to run the ship's office in his absence and developed a comprehensive collection of Standard Operating Procedures to increase efficiency.

- Led a section of 8 Second Class Petty Officers in the performance of weekly personnel and unit inspections which reinforced goals, improved performance, and increased morale.

- Led a team of Sailors in the structural realignment and maintenance of over 3,000 square feet of patient care spaces resulting in an estimated Command cost savings of $50,000

- Led and trained seven personnel during our participation in three global exercises; dramatically expanded their skill set and confidence.

- Led by coaching, always providing positive reinforcement to motivate personnel to improve, both professionally and personally.

- Led by example while executing over 30 challenging training operations; conducted thorough readiness training drills to ensure his Sailors were always prepared for any eventuality.

- Led workcenter to highest PRT average in the unit; raised workcenter average by 40%!

- Maintained an outstanding 95% retention rate and an astonishing 80% advancement rate.

- Mature leader. Won't compromise standards; enforced highest USFLTFORCOM standards of conduct

- MENTOR AND LEADER. As Senior Enlisted Leader, he solved many housing, medical, and personnel issues.

- Organized a goal-oriented office team and encouraged team input to reduce the number of administrative problems.

- Organized a team for the March of Dimes 10K Walk America and raised over $2,000 to combat birth defects

- Out of her 5 personal protégés, she produced the Junior Sailor of the Year, two Junior Sailors of the Quarter, and a Blue Jacket of the Quarter.

- Performed exceptionally well while leading seaman in difficult, constantly evolving combat operations

- Petty Officer Gonzalez's experience and devotion to mission success continues to inspire her peers and promote Navy pride and professionalism.

- Petty Officer Jones is directly responsible for turning around the production effectiveness of the recruiting station, resulting in zero attrition since assuming responsibility as RinC.

- Proven management skills set him apart from his peers; transformed workcenter from sub-standard to compliant or better. Promote ASAP!

- Provided extraordinary leadership to personnel, keeping a relentless focus on professional development that resulted in one advancement to Senior Chief and two advancements to Chief.

- Reported aboard as Chief of the Boat and immediately improved the crew's morale and performance. A genuine leader, he has an innate ability to facilitate teamwork and motivate his peers and subordinates to achieve ship's goals.

- Revived the unit's Navy Family Accountability and Assessment System (NFAAS) program. Aggressive follow-up and adherence to standards reduced errors and increased readiness for unexpected events; best program on base

- Selfless Mentor. His counseling and leadership resulted in his only military subordinate earning Sailor of the Year for DISA-EUR and his efforts on several boards produced both SOY DISA-EUR and Sailor of the Year DISA. Puts new meaning into the phrase, "taking care of Sailors".

- Senior Chief Smith is a staunch advocate of tradition, loyalty, and service. His unwavering support of the chain of command, firm enforcement of military standards, and equitable treatment of subordinates has optimized morale and promoted teamwork and mission accomplishment.

- Sets the example by winning the respect of the local national community and treating detainees with dignity and consideration

- Shared years of maintenance experience with LCAC Engineer trainees and saw immediate and readily apparent improvement in repair turn-around time

- She coached a skilled team of seven Petty Officers to produce regular and comprehensive After Action Reports for senior leadership which identified problem areas and improved group readiness and performance.

- Spearheaded a USS CONSTITUTION-like CPO inductee event aboard the USS MISSOURI; promoted pride in Navy service

- Spearheaded the overall push for Anti-Terrorism and VBSS readiness by providing high risk training to over 100 armed sentries annually during the SRFB course held onboard

- Standards and professional competence generated immediate confidence and improved subordinate morale

- STANDOUT MENTOR. His "Stay Navy" attitude was directly responsible for attaining 100% retention.

- Stellar CPO who leads by example; an invaluable asset to the Naval Service Training Command

- Stepped up as Acting Leading Chief Petty Officer following the unexpected mobilization of his LCPO.

- Stepped up to the plate in the absence of the CPO. Performed leadership duties in a decisive and positive manner with exceptional results.

- SUCCESSFUL MENTOR. Consistently gets the best from the best. Three Pacific Network Managers of the Month, Two PNM of the Quarter, and One DISA NCO of the year!

- Superb leader. Molded an inexperienced workcenter into an efficient, cohesive team, greatly increasing productivity and morale.

- SUPERIOR LEADER! United a team of joint service NCOs and 14 civilians to man a 24-hour command center providing up-to-the-minute, real-time management of all critical data communications traversing EUCOM. Analyzed impact of circuit outages and directed restorals based on priority and close coordination with organizational Commander.

- Team builder. Ensured the incremental completion of long and short range training plans producing 30 divisional qualifications and enhancing the flexibility of a 24 hour watch bill. Encouraged and supported maximum participation in MWR events, sports, and unit picnics

- The cornerstone of our team, taking care of our Sailors is his top concern.

- United a team of active duty and reserve Sailors into one cohesive and productive organization

- Unparalleled enthusiasm; possesses an out-in-front leadership style and the attributes of today's model CPO and leader

- USS Bainbridge has the best retention rate in the Fleet as a direct result of his hard work, perseverance, and insight.

Training

- Accomplished 270 of 325 qualification tasks; 77% completed on three airframes; 25% ahead of peers

- As Command Financial Specialist, developed a heightened sense of financial awareness and responsibility throughout the command through education and counseling that helped sailors avoid financial hardships.

- As Command trainer, ensured 100% on-time PQS completion and the qualification of 5 zone supervisors and 15 Recruiters-in-Charge.

- As IA liaison, he trained 22 personnel, all 100% qualified to deploy in support of the Global War on Terrorism with maximum support and readiness.

- As the Damage Control training team coordinator, he led the Bainbridge through two Ultra-S certifications and achieved MOB-D certification at Ultra-C, a milestone achieved well ahead of schedule.

- As the Department Training Petty Officer, his comprehensive training program resulted in the qualification of five new Coxswains, directly improving Command readiness.

- As training manager, she obtained three scarce regional AGS training slots; prevented delay in personnel qualifications and increased readiness.

- Continuously reevaluated training; his efforts ensured that SEABEEs had the most up to date training available based on real world threats and returning unit debriefs.

- CM2 Smith provided over 40 hours of urgent on-the-job training to four mechanics, who, with no previous construction experience, were assigned maintenance responsibility for five Caterpillar D7Gs.

- Demonstrating skill and professionalism, he helped train and qualify 20 personnel in the use and correction of navigational charts and instruments.

- Designed training program that improved the skills of subordinate observation teams resulting in a 33% increase in capabilities during operations

- Developed a cross-training program and self-directed work atmosphere that improved watch member productivity during all shifts

- Developed and implemented a phased training program; reduced required training time of newly assigned personnel by six months

- Developed training program that capitalized on civilian depot maintenance experience raising Sailor qualifications and reducing need for outside assistance

- Drastically reduced generator failures across Kandahar Air Field by instructing 7 Soldiers on the proper maintenance of diesel generators

- Empowered over 100 Sailors by training them to generate their own AT/ADT order requests and travel claims

- Enriched the experience of her students by careful analysis of their qualifications and work history

- Ensured over 5000 deploying Seabees were prepared for construction and combat operations in four AORs spanning the globe

- Enterprising and motivated instructor, achieved MTS 6 months ahead of standards

- Excellent leader. Supervised computer renewal of four classrooms, replacing 80 workstations and component hardware and software with no loss of training days

- Expert Electronic Standards Section trainer; trained six technicians on section's most complex test equipment

- Focused on improvement, she established a collateral duty at-sea PAO training plan that increased participation in a waning program.

- He trained and qualified 11 newly assigned personnel at several watchstations to improve watchstander efficiency and readiness.

- He was responsible for the addition of CPR and First Aid to the courses for six different rates and trained over 1500 Sailors in life saving skills.

- Helped reduce attrition rates in the Basic Reconnaissance Course and multiplied force effectiveness by directly supporting a critically under-manned MOS for the Special Operations Community

- Her efforts proved integral to the recertification process of 24 shipboard cranes and cargo loading appendages.

- His commitment to high quality training and operations lead to the safe completion of three nuclear refueling missions and over 500 anti-terrorism operations.

- His experience and mentorship were vital in the training and development of over 5,000 students in preparation for Fleet duty.

- His high expectations during Land Navigation, Close Quarters Battle, and Land Warfare culminated in a safe and effective block of training.

- His on-going documentation of lessons learned from his years of experience as a senior officer has proven to be invaluable in the development of junior personnel.

- His vast experience and valuable technical expertise ensured the training he provided led to crews and warships ready for tasking for the Global War on Terror.

- HM3 Smith spearheaded the medical support for the Marine Corps Mountain Warfare Training Challenge. He put together a thorough and in-depth plan in order to provide quality support for all active duty and civilian participants and meet all contingencies.

- Identified and resolved software incompatibility issue which threatened to prevent class operation. Experience, knowledge, and foresight prevented class delays.

- Managed the course curriculum and served as Safety Observer for the Damage Control Wet Trainer; careful oversight prevented injuries

- Outstanding Instructor. Ensured smooth operation of classroom instruction, curriculum development, and course administration. Donated over 200 hours of off-duty instruction and extra study for 40 students and lowered attrition rate to zero

- Provided unprecedented technical expertise and managerial insight to students assigned to the Marine combat training battalion

- Prepared work center personnel for their qualification evaluations; increased work center pass rate by 50%, now leads the DESRON

- Provided 22 hours of flight crew instruction; taught 40 members respiratory protection/QNFT. His professionalism was vital to successful deployment operations.

- Reorganized the Line Division training program so well that his workcenter received the Workcenter Professionalism Award for 1st quarter of 2009

- Resourceful; obtained two scarce Remote Mine Hunting System training slots; saved $7,000, increased Minesweeper personnel qualification

- Revised examination procedures for submarine crew members; incorporated low light requirements to more accurately tailor training

- Scheduled course dates for officer and enlisted military members to attend; maximum use of available slots

- She demonstrated remarkable resourcefulness in developing and presenting the AWS course during multiple speaking engagements at two Command facilities.

- Spearheaded campaign to increase training plan efficiency; assumed responsibility for incorporating all training inputs and training documentation

- Trained 12 newly assigned personnel on crisis response procedures; significantly enhanced war-fighting abilities

- Trained new personnel on Document Exploitation (DOCEX) team in the Multinational Division-Southern Area of Operations. All members shift-qualified ahead of schedule, increased the AO's exploitation potential by 50%

- Trained over 1,000 students from fleet personnel, Naval reserves, NROTC, and other military and civil organizations in high risk live fire fighting and damage control

- Trained, established roles for six Battlestaff watch officers in preparation for EUCOM's largest exercise; 99% successful tactical comm supporting over 20,000 troops

- Volunteered to organize and review training records, his proactive analysis revealed several qualification problem areas which led to a revised training program and ultimately produced the best overall certification rate in the group.

- With incomparable skill and ingenuity, Petty Officer Gonzalez trained over 2000 sailors on 16 ships during all phases of training over an aggressive 55 week schedule.

- Within three months of checking onboard he was quickly trained, 100% qualified, and deployed to Iraq in support of Operation Iraqi Freedom.

Recognition

Recommending someone for an award is not the only way to recognize top performance. Often, recognition by our peers and superiors during the course of our daily work is worth far more than a medal. Note that recognition is similar to stratification comments and more examples can be found in that section.

- A recognized authority, he is routinely sought out by other Petty Officers for advice and guidance.

- A recognized subject matter expert, he made precise recommendations that were critical to successful tactical planning, situational awareness, and safety of personnel and equipment.

- As Leading Petty Officer, received Bravo Zulu during mock Joint Commission Inspection receiving zero hits on the sterilization, storage, and procedural processes of all equipment.

- As the sole trainer for 9 nuclear medicine technologists and 15 students, she is the go-to person for matters related to positron emission tomography.

- Awarded the National Defense Service Medal for support of Operation DESERT SHIELD/DESERT STORM

- Best in command! USNAVCENT's Financial Management Specialist of the Year for 2002!

- Chief Smith played a critical role in the first successful engagement utilizing the Navy's newest air-to-ground weapons delivery system.

- Displaying exceptional skill and resourcefulness, his efforts resulted in his selection as Junior Sailor of the Year 2010.

- Due to his extensive experience and background, he was personally requested to instruct ATKWINGSLANT's MTIP Corrosion Control course.

- Exceptional instructor. Handpicked by Command Master Chief to instruct new Third Class Petty Officers.

- ET3 Smith has shown leadership and technical abilities far surpassing that of a Third Class Petty Officer.

- His contract and acquisition experience, including firm fixed price and time and materials contracts, places him at the forefront of Supply Corps Acquisition Officer activity.

- His dedication earned recognition as Great Lakes Instructor of the Quarter and Junior Sailor of the Quarter.

- His efforts behind the scenes toward the resolution of these issues are seldom seen or recognized but the results are enjoyed by all

- Nominated as Helicopter Maritime Strike Squadron 71 Junior Sailor of the Quarter, 2nd Quarter 2010

- Outstanding professional expertise. Handpicked from an elite group of First Class Petty Officers to certify squadron aircraft as safe for flight.

- Petty Officer Smith was personally requested to oversee the Pearl Harbor income tax assistance program.

- Received accolades from C5RA assessors for the superior performance of weapons, radar, and data systems

- Received Letter of Appreciation from NAS Oceana Family Services Center for VITS Program volunteer services

- Received Letter of Commendation from RADM Sims for actions in support of COMSECONDFLT and USCENTCOM during pre-deployment planning for Operation DESERT STORM

- Selected ahead of all USS Ronald Reagan CPOs for Northrop Grumman Research Company Quality Assurance (QA) program

- Singled out to assist the local security group activity in the installation, activation, and testing of new security monitoring equipment.

- Their recruiting team wrote 55 contracts in a year which led to their recognition as FY-10 Medium Station of the Year.

- Top Seaman! Selected as the NAVSURFWARCEN Sailor of the Quarter for the 3rd Quarter 2009

- Undisputed authority; chosen to conduct AMW/MOB certifications on 5 most critical SURFLANT ships, delivered most thorough and complete review to date

Stratification

Describing someone as first out of 10 or second out of seven isn't the only way to compare a person's performance to their peers. Almost everyone is the best at something within a certain group. Below are examples, some more subtle than others, of showing superior ability, even if it's not officially recognized.

- Asked for by name to assist the Fire Control section

- At Tactical Application and the Global Command and Control System Maritime classes, he was voted top student.

- CPO Jones is solely responsible for the overall management of this Squadron's flawless Hazardous Waste program.

- Chosen to represent the unit at the annual conference

- Displayed superior teamwork and in-depth knowledge. As the only Quality Assurance Inspector in the weapons department, he was singularly responsible for the timely completion of 15 Quality Assurance work packages.

- FC1 Smith was the point man aboard the Bainbridge for over 1200 hours expended on data collection, cause analysis, and repair of the chronic waveguide arcing problem.

- Hand-picked to become Maintenance Control qualified and certified to release aircraft safe for flight

- Hand-picked to lead a joint theater team which discovered, targeted, and performed damage assessment on hundreds of key targets; critical to mission success

- He was chosen to reevaluate and monitor Patient Care activity and establish process improvement initiatives to improve the quality of Patient Care and ensure the best treatment was provided for fleet members.

- His program was one of only two programs to reach their goals out of 13 departments.

- My number one Mobility Line troop; can always be counted on to ensure compliance with requirements

- Petty Officer Gonzalez is the lead on receipt, organization, and stowage of over $10,000 in critical repair parts.

- Petty Officer Smith achieved unparalleled success in the performance of his duties.

- Requested by name to head up our most critical program

- Selected by Fuels Officer to head up all high profile and difficult missions

- Selected from among his peers to serve as Auxiliary Division LCPO for newly-commissioned Arleigh Burke class destroyer

- Singled out for the Leading Chief Petty Officer Leadership Course over other CPOs

- Standout performer. Selectively chosen to perform duties as flight line coordinator, a billet normally assigned to a Chief Petty Officer.

- Subject matter expert; the only Department member capable of programming the Systems bridge

- SUPERB ADMINISTRATOR. Selected over peers to coordinate the squadron's classified material and high value pack-up and transport for the Weapons Detachment

- The driving force behind the Squadron's outstanding Hazardous Material/Hazardous Waste program

- The expert on aircraft electrical and airframe systems. Expertise and knowledge are continually called upon by both military and contractors

- The only Air Wing Damage Control Petty Officer to qualify as CVW-7 3M PQS Qualifier

- The only Second Class holding an LPO position, she mentored junior Sailors resulting in overall advancement and selection of two Sailors for Sailor of the Quarter.

- The squadron's go-to man for networking issues

Community Service

- Aided in the success of the facility excellence program; 100+ hours of base beautification; enhanced installation appearance/quality of life

- Chaired Operation White Christmas; planned and organized the entire program and raised over $10,000 for 55 needy enlisted families

- Civic Minded. Dedicated 12 hours mentoring 10 youth in key areas of responsibility and professional development

- Coached youth soccer and track, raised funds for the USN Birthday Ball, a hallmark event for over 1000 sailors and their families; forged deckplate pride

- Community Involved. As volunteer Block Watch Captain in the Neighborhood Watch Program, he coordinated watches with neighbors and local police.

- COMMUNITY INVOLVEMENT. Coach for youth athletics baseball and football teams; bettered base environment

- COMMUNITY INVOLVEMENT. Organized several projects for Waipahu elementary school raising over $6,000 for needed improvements

- Community Involvement. Spent off-duty hours coaching advanced soccer league for Norfolk families

- Community leader. Volunteered over 40 hours for the base blood drive and the Seattle Seafair; active FCPOA member who set the tempo for peers and junior Sailors

- COMMUNITY SERVICE. Volunteered as co-chairman of Patch Barracks Community Crime Watch Organization

- COMMUNITY SERVICE. Worked over 200 off-duty hours renovating Pearl Harbor Calvary Chapel; example enriched services

- Conscientious community member. Devoted over 200 hours of personal time to community youth and senior citizen programs in San Diego County

- Conscientious volunteer and community leader. Vice-President of Squadron First Class Petty Officer Association and Cub Scout Den Leader

- Counseled 20 children in the Naval Forces Marianas AWANA (Approved Workmen Are Not Ashamed) program

- Firmly supports community; active volunteer for community "clean the bay" days and construction of "kids cove" playground

- He was personally responsible for coordinating two blood drives and the joint-base Misawa City "United We Can" food drive.

- Heartfelt leadership! Invited three Norfolk shipmates for Thanksgiving and Christmas day meals; genuine troop caretaker

- Humanitarian! Gave 40 nurturing hours to Sasebo base animal shelter; provided care for over 30 abandoned animals

- Implemented all Navy Equal Opportunity safeguards, established 100% contact, ensured mission accomplishment

- Minimized Navy expenses by supporting the self-help renovation of San Antonio NOSC

- Motivated team player; contributed off duty time and effort to support unit's self-help project; saved estimated $30,000

- Organized beautification project for Pearl Harbor elementary school, raised over $3,000 for new classroom furniture

- Participated in 8-hour Adopt-a-Highway cleanup; removed 200 pounds of refuse, fostered community/Navy alliance

- Participated in humanitarian actions in Guam and East Timor and Operation Enduring Freedom, helped to liberate an oppressed nation

- Petty Officer Jones participated in two COMREL projects and the self-help installation of two basketball goals for the NSA Youth Center.

- Radiates energy and extreme enthusiasm while supporting activities at the NAS Jacksonville community chapel

- Sacrificed 100 hours of limited personal time to coach Virginia Beach High School weight training class

- Selected as and served as MWR Treasurer

- Spearheaded youth/adult annual football game; improved morale for families and ship's military members

- Strong, positive drive toward helping others in need; continually supported Guam's Santa Rita Foundation; gifts ensured children had access to food, shelter, medical care, education, and a supportive environment

- Supported the Combined Federal Campaign, participated in ship's annual Habitat for Humanity charity

- Tireless volunteer. Devoted over 80 hours to community youth and senior citizen programs in San Diego County

- Vice President of Aomori elementary PTO; spearheaded fund raisers and raised $2,000 for school events, field trips

- Visited 2 Philippine orphanages; donated over 40 hours labor on new building; solidified community support

- Volunteered 8 hours with the Meals on Wheels program of Fort Worth Texas

- Volunteered as phone bank operator during Easter Seal telethon; surpassed its goal and raised $30,000

- Volunteered several off-duty days for events such as the 5k Race for the Cure and the Virginia Beach Fourth of July Celebration

Management/Mentorship

- A brilliant manager who is committed to total quality. Through his guidance and technical expertise he was directly responsible for the line division receiving grades of Outstanding on work center quarterly audits.

- After an inspection grade of Marginal, his dedication toward training and realigning administration and operations yielded an ORI report of Outstanding in 6 out of 8 categories.

- AGGRESSIVE SUPERVISOR. Trained an inexperienced ordnance crew during the short-notice preparation for the demanding Conventional Weapons Technical Proficiency Inspection, earning a grade of 90.5

- As Camp Czar and Senior Enlisted Advisor, he worked tirelessly to give every Sailor the chance they deserved and the opportunities they earned.

- As Command Career Counselor, he oversaw 12 career development boards while his retention efforts resulted in 15 service member re-enlistments.

- As Operations Chief for the Combined Task Force 56, he integrated the efforts of a diverse group of military professionals and focused their efforts to accomplish their mission 6 months ahead of schedule.

- As the 25 NCR logistics Leading Petty Officer, he demonstrated a unique ability to motivate personnel to perform to the best of their abilities.

- As the LCPO for Naval Branch Health Clinic Yuma, she mentored 30 sailors which resulted in 4 promotions, 4 reenlistments, and one Bluejacket of the Quarter.

- As the lead diver, Petty Officer Smith used his leadership abilities to bring a multi-organizational dive team together as a team to successfully accomplish their objective.

- As the NCR logistics Leading Petty Officer, he supervised the gear issue and retrograde for over 2000 personnel transiting through Camp Moreell, Kuwait.

- As the newly appointed administrator of over $2M in assets, he led a 5 man team in the refurbishment of three buildings, one armory, and five boats.

- By his diligence and hard work, he directly contributed to mission accomplishment and increased staff morale.

- Chief Gonzalez displayed exceptional professional agility while leading his reserve unit in support of Sealift Logistics Command Europe operations and Military Sealift Fleet Support.

- Chief Jones expertly led 130 personnel in six production work centers completing over 2,500 critical maintenance actions and 200 special inspections accounting for 2,550 man hours on ten supporting HH-60H aircraft.

- Chief Petty Officer Smith's inspirational leadership and technical expertise guided support personnel to exceed all goals during the land warfare unit level training.

- Chief Smith's management of four HH-60H aircraft and 35 maintenance personnel launched 120 successful combat missions in support of SOCPAC during Operation Iraqi Freedom with a 99% completion rate.

- Compiled detailed after-action reports that were key to improving future deployment operations throughout the fleet

- Coordinated, prioritized, and managed all Camp Krutke maintenance projects from cradle to grave with no time lost to accidents, safety violations, or quality discrepancies

- DEDICATED MENTOR! As Command Mentor, she skillfully matched all sailors with competent mentors and facilitated the personal and professional development of all members.

- Demonstrating superb leadership and expert technique, he facilitated a team effort while setting a phenomenal production pace that resulted in the attainment of numerous command goals for the first time ever.

- Demonstrating technical expertise and outstanding leadership, he molded his division of six junior Sailors into outstanding Fire Control technicians, spending more than 200 hours of onboard training on fire control operations and target motion analysis.

- Developed a cross-training program and self-directed work environment that improved employee productivity by 55%

- Developed a training program that capitalized on civilian depot maintenance experience raising Sailor qualifications and reducing the need for outside assistance

- Developed and maintained an intensive physical fitness program that improved morale and increased PRT averages by 40%

- Diligent planning and inter-office coordination reduced work order back log to lowest in 10 years and launched fleet with largest complement of aircraft to date

- Diligent contingency planning and coordination resulted in the efficient restoral of over 1500 network outages providing 100% always-on comm service to deployed users!

- Directed the Department's on-the-job training program which resulted in 6 sailors receiving their certification ahead of schedule

- During his tenure, he completed all projects and assigned tasks ahead of schedule and under budget while maintaining a very high degree of quality and safety.

- Effective manager who runs an efficient and productive workcenter as evidenced by two consecutive Quality Assurance Audits which garnered grades of Outstanding

- Efficiently prepared for an East PAC deployment. Ensured the department was always stocked and ready for immediate deployment and sustained performance at sea

- Exhibited outstanding leadership and maturity as the Electrical Branch Leading Petty Officer

- Facilitated the success of two zones, leading one to become Zone of the Year and the other to achieve over 100% after previously struggling to make goals

- GYSGT Smith planned and executed physical fitness, close order drill, and leadership training designed to prepare midshipmen for the rigors of Naval service.

- He completed 55 performance evaluations, 75 items of formal correspondence, and maintained 100% accountability of personnel via official muster.

- He ensured the professional, administrative, and physical readiness of the unit's members while experiencing unprecedented success in the completion of assigned tasks.

- He led and trained 25 military and 25 civilian staff in the successful execution of several highly visible evolutions, including the Change of Command and Inspector General's visit.

- Helped stand up the Fleet Readiness Center; established capabilities and priorities that produced immediate movement toward goals

- Her superb managerial skills pushed our clinic to win the TRICARE Regional Access Award for 2 consecutive years.

- His continuous devotion to the training and professional growth of others increased overall readiness and created the model for all competing units to emulate.

- His leadership contributed to an impressive crewman boot camp throughout the maritime expeditionary security force community.

- His proactive leadership style was particularly effective in the planning and perfect execution of the Phase II installation.

- His steadfast commitment to the personal and professional growth of his Sailors facilitated the recognition of one of his Sailors as Sailor of the Quarter and another for being nominated for Maintenance Professional of the Year.

- Increased productivity and morale in the Department as demonstrated by two consecutive Quality Assurance Audits with outstanding results

- Invested in his organization, he passionately seeks improvement in all areas of endeavor.

- Managed 30-member workcenter in direct support of U.S. Naval Network and Space Operations Command and exceeded all assigned goals!

- Managed a complex mix of terrestrial and satellite communications links to provide reliable service to over 100,000 military personnel in the Persian Gulf.

- Master Chief Smith coordinated manpower, operational requirements, watch-bills, and personnel assignments in support of deployment to Singapore for exercise Pacific Reach. His leadership and expertise were directly responsible for the unprecedented success of the exercise.

- Mentored sailors. Superior ability to develop non rate personnel into competent armorer custodians who were responsible for the success of AirDet armory during FEX.

- Molded a junior division into an unstoppable and cohesive team

- Oversaw critical operations in the Information Collection Section and was responsible for over 200 Requests for Information in less than a week during heightened operations. Section's efforts and dedication was integral to the intelligence effort and mission success.

- Petty Officer Jones' leadership experience and devotion to mission success continues to inspire his peers and promotes Navy pride and professionalism.

- Petty Officer Jones presided over 250 evolutions while serving as Assistant Watch Officer with impressive results.

- Petty Officer Smith consistently demonstrated mature judgment and keen foresight in all matters of administration.

- Petty Officer Smith demonstrated dynamic leadership ability in the supervision of 5 military and 3 civilian personnel which increased the effectiveness of operations within the Admin Department.

- Petty Officer Smith established a new station, from the ground up, attaining full mission capability and superior results in the first year of operation.

- Petty Officer Smith took a functional but declining supply department and, using his talent and hard work, turned it into a productive work place where Sailors enjoyed their work.

- Petty Officer Smith's duties as Career Counselor contributed to 27 reenlistments, 2 cross ratings, and the manning award for Point Mugu.

- Petty Officer Smith's inspirational leadership and technical expertise guided Norfolk Naval Shipyard to exceed all operational goals for FY09 and FY10.

- Prepared a supply level for over $250,000 worth of equipment and purchased over $20,000 in patient education materials and equipment exceeding the requirements of Fiscal Year OPTAR.

- Provided outstanding legal and professional counsel to both Task Force and Department members.

- Senior Chief Jones' superior leadership, judgment, and management were crucial to the safe completion of the replenishment effort.

- Senior Chief Smith displayed exceptional leadership and outstanding resourcefulness by supervising more than 500 man hours of mishap-free underway training and the expenditure of more than 50k rounds in weapons sustainment and qualifications.

- Skillful administrator and manager. Guided work center to grades of Outstanding on AIRLANT inspections and quarterly audits.

- Superbly handled all personnel matters in his role as Senior Enlisted Advisor. Provided intelligent counsel to Commander and staff on a wide range of issues including crew morale, personnel planning, and ship employment.

- Superior oversight. As NCOIC, he meticulously managed the daily review and integration of five data networks and ten workstations. He was the driving force behind the successful implementation of the NATO Unclassified Network which was critical for coordinating joint operations with multi-national coalition partners.

- Supervised a long overdue and complicated preventive maintenance inspection on Lago Di Patria satellite equipment. Supervised and trained five technicians on measurements, adjustments, lubrication, and alignments. Completed tests within allotted downtime; ensured 100% reliable communications

- Under his supervision, the supply department outfitted and retrograded tactical gear for over 1500 personnel transiting through Camp Moreell en route to Iraq and Afghanistan.

- While serving as section Leading Chief Petty Officer for Harbor Patrol unit, NSA Bahrain, Chief Smith supervised, trained, and mentored 50 sailors while flawlessly conducting day to day operations within and around the AOR.

- Worked directly with Army SECFOR to integrate Navy and Army forces and ensured all members of CTG 56.5 were properly trained to stand multiple posts with their Army counterparts

Self-Help Projects

- Aided in facility excellence program; worked over 100 hours for base beautification; enhanced installation appearance/quality of life

- Dedicated 90 off-duty hours to upgrade the integrated bridge system and correct faulty cabling and software problems enabling the successful completion of sea trials and NavCert

- Directed the completion of a 500 meter road for the new Kuwaiti camp that saved the host nation more than $800,000

- Displayed exceptional creativity and innovative use of personnel and resources as rehab coordinator onboard USS Bainbridge, making workcenter spaces squadron ready

- Displaying unrivaled administrative abilities, Petty Officer Smith was instrumental in the renovation of the 100-personnel administrative department.

- Minimized Navy expenses by supporting the self-help renovation of NOSC San Antonio

- Motivated team player; contributed off duty time and effort to support unit's self-help project and saved est $30,000

- Participated in the reorganization and upgrade of Pass & ID facility on off-duty time; saved Navy over $5,000 in labor costs

- Petty Officer Jones' masonry skills had a major impact on the Battalion's #1 self-help priority, completing the foundation 30 days ahead of schedule.

- Planned restroom addition and construction at Group Flight facility. Conducted cost analysis, recommended in-house project; his efforts saved the Navy over $200,000

- Repaired 11 bulkhead holes, repaired 22 feet of deck edge and rebuilt 2 flushing reducing stations saving the Navy an estimated $100,000 in repair costs

- Worked over 200 off-duty hours renovating Pearl Harbor Calvary Chapel

Derogatory Comments

- A remarkable lack of ability to execute his duties and depends on others for help

- Allows the pressures of family issues to affect her performance. Recommend release from duties and counseling until such time she can resume work without endangering others.

- Although PO Smith is always respectful and courteous to everyone encountered, he shows little to no interest toward this type of duty, and has failed to meet the requirements for Level II Patrol Officer.

- An outstanding technical resource but needs to work on tact and communication skills

- Avoids responsibility and is a negative influence on his section

- Cannot be depended on and is always late for shift. Recommend...

- Cannot be relied upon to maintain production rate in the absence of supervision

- Cannot be trusted to oversee safe delivery of...must be supervised at all times

- Cannot work with his peers and is counter-productive

- Demonstrated a lack of skill or knowledge in most of his duties. He does not comply with instructions and is a threat to the safety of this ship Recommend discharge at earliest opportunity

- Demonstrates a serious lack of integrity and poor judgment which highlights the reckless personal choices that he makes in his personal life

- Despite encouragement and efforts of peers, cannot qualify for duty and fails to make effort to improve

- Despite increasing assistance and training, he continues to have serious difficulty completing assigned tasks; recommend reclassification

- Despite the best efforts of trainers on and off-duty, was unsuccessful in...

- Despite repeated counseling, unsatisfactory behavior created a distraction within the Division and interfered with good order and discipline.

- Did not meet expectations in...

- Displayed little regard for Navy core values and service with honor

- Displays a remarkable and consistent lack of initiative or enthusiasm and is the subject of frequent counseling

- Doesn't put forward the effort required to become proficient in her duties

- Doesn't realize the critical importance of following orders and may endanger this command

- Failed to acquire the necessary skills and attributes to...

- Failed to maintain standards and allowed his workcenter rating to decrease from Excellent to Satisfactory

- Failed to meet Strike Group standards and should not be retained

- Failed to render the proper respect and was subject to Captain's Mast twice. SN3 Smith has not made any effort to change his behavior during this reporting period and is not fit for retention.

- Failed to take advantage of opportunities to advance...

- Fails to understand the importance of his duties, takes advantage of every situation to avoid responsibility

- Fails to use time wisely

- Had poor rapport with his subordinates and was ineffectual in supervision or delegation of responsibilities

- Has the potential to be an excellent technician but is often careless with...

- His failure to follow orders led to the loss of his security clearance and now section is undermanned and unable to meet quota

- His performance was below average and he is in immediate need of retraining.

- His performance was inaccurate at best and wildly incorrect when under stress.

- Is a capable Yeoman but fails to use her abilities to the fullest

- Is indifferent to suggestions for advancement and misses many opportunities for learning

- Is often unaware of operational picture and his section members are left unsupervised

- Is uncooperative when corrected and displays a consistent lack of interest in Department's goals

- Lacks enthusiasm in his duties and has no pride in his performance

- Lacks experience and fails to understand the importance of advancement

- Lacks initiative and managerial skills

- Lacks respect for chain of command and needs improvement in peer communications

- Lagged behind contemporaries in every aspect of training

- Leadership and managerial skills need improvement to qualify for next rank.

- Mediocre staff skills contributed to mediocre results during INSURV

- Negatively affected our state of readiness by...

- Not fit for this type of activity, exhibits a negative attitude and should be disqualified

- Not focused, sometimes distracted, her accuracy rate was the lowest in the shop

- Performance is erratic and undependable

- Presents an unprofessional appearance and lacks military bearing

- Probably the worst performer in our Command

- Repeatedly refused suggestions to attend counseling until her problems escalated to the point of making her unfit for duty

- Reported to work under the influence of alcohol and was unable to execute his duties as...

- Resists suggestions for improvement and actively works against the orders of his superiors

- Seaman Smith is encouraged to find an aspect of his job he can enjoy and take pride in before being recommended to the next rank.

- Superb performance but uniform and bearing do not meet standards and will hold this Sailor back

- Twice cited for disrespect toward an officer

- Unable to adjust to sea duty or the diverse demands of deployment

- Unable to report to work on time and needs constant supervision. Retention is not advised.

- Was and is negligent in meeting his responsibilities causing numerous obstacles to mission accomplishment

- Was disciplined for assault and his off-duty actions make him unfit for duty

- Was entrusted with our most critical and essential tasks but disappointed his mentors

- Was an ineffective leader and provided no useful guidance

- When reminded, can be a very motivated individual

- Will not use off-duty time for study or self-improvement; fails to advance in qualification

- YN1 Smith is uncooperative with leadership and fails to understand the difference between "taking care of troops" and following orders. His combative attitude is counter-productive and a liability to this Command.

- YN3 Smith has been given every tool for success yet he blatantly discards them all. He possesses a self destructive demeanor that spreads like a cancer to newly assigned Sailors.

Closing Comments

The Eval's summary or closing comments must sum up the impression that the writer is trying to convey about the person being evaluated. Normally, one to three lines are used at the bottom of the Comments on Performance block to summarize the tone of the report and provide a promotion statement. It shouldn't take more than two lines to express approval and if three are used, it makes it appear as if the subject of the eval doesn't have many accomplishments. Below are examples of successful closing statements.

A competent leader with potential. Possesses the necessary skills to effectively achieve any objective. His leadership style instills enthusiasm in all who work for him. Excellent speaking and writing skills. Wears his uniform with pride. Recommended for advancement.

A consummate professional and unrivaled technical expert. Petty Officer Smith is a gifted, inspirational leader and manager. Demands and receives maximum support from subordinates through invigorating leadership and direct supervision. Possesses unlimited potential. Maintains a clean and neat appearance. Most strongly recommended for advancement to Chief Petty Officer.

A consummate professional whose commitment to excellence continues to be the catalyst for success. Steadfastly loyal to this command and the Navy. Exceptional communicator both written and orally. Will excel in any demanding position. Managerial and leadership abilities are second to none. Has my strongest endorsement for selection to Chief Petty Officer and all programs leading to a commission.

A CONSUMMATE PROFESSIONAL. Has proven himself a dedicated leader who thrives on challenge. A total team player with a cooperative spirit that contributes to the high morale in the work center. Exceptional counseling and communicative skills. Most strongly recommended for advancement to Chief Petty Officer.

A dynamic Senior Enlisted Advisor (SEA), he facilitated communication between the ranks and increased overall satisfaction at work. None better at what they do! Should already be a CHIEF. PROMOTE IMMEDIATELY!

A positive leadership example that consistently brought out the best in her subordinates. Promote now!

A positive, can-do attitude; an example to his peers and subordinates

A proven leader and team builder. Select now for only the most challenging duties as a MMCPO.

A rare combination of efficiency and initiative, this Sailor provided leadership and the best possible environment for success. Overdue for promotion to Chief!

A rare combination of leadership and humility, he has the strength to lead but is mature enough to recognize his weaknesses.

A rock-solid performer; consistently provides high-caliber maintenance and technical direction

A section leader with unmatched dedication to duty and personal performance. Promote now to PO1!

A superb radio operator. Definitely promote this outstanding and professional operator.

A superb technician; highly motivated and dependable; consistently delivered quality service to customers; promote.

A TOTAL PROFESSIONAL. Possesses the leadership skills and talent to succeed in challenging positions. Encourages innovative thinking among his subordinates and fosters professional and personal growth. Displays impressive military bearing and appearance. Highly recommended for advancement to Chief Petty Officer.

A true professional who's always in the middle of our most critical processes. Promote immediately!

A world-class CPO who leads by example; a solid professional ready for increased responsibility; promote!

Aboard for only six months, SA Smith is already 75% qualified on work center maintenance training tasks. Promote when ready.

Absolute TOP NOTCH in every respect. The only E-6 to attain the title of Senior Watch Officer and a leader in whom I place extraordinary trust!

Absolutely superior Petty Officer; excelled in job performance, community service, and leadership. Promote at once!

AC1 Smith has demonstrated his capability and grown beyond his duties as Petty Officer First Class. Support the Department and the Navy by advancing to Chief now.

An earnest and capable seaman, she exhibits discipline in working towards completion of qualification training.

An enthusiastic Hospital Corpsman with a can-do attitude. P.O. Jones is always willing to accept more challenging tasks with greater responsibility. Promote to Chief now.

An extremely dedicated hard-charger. A top-notch professional who exudes confidence in every undertaking. Seeks greater responsibility. Highly motivated with unlimited potential. Fully supports the Navy's Equal Opportunity Program. Excellent communication skills. Impressive military bearing and appearance. Most strongly recommended for advancement to Chief Petty Officer.

An exceptional Petty Officer with unlimited potential. He has demonstrated his dedication to mission accomplishment by a positive, can-do attitude and continuous self-improvement. Urgently recommended for advancement and retention in the US Naval service.

An incomparable team player! Propelled unit to win 2009 AFCEA Copernicus Award; Early Promote!

AO2 Jones is a standout performer who maintains the trust and confidence of his peers and chain of command. His relentless drive to complete all tasks from start to finish with unrivaled results make him a juggernaut amongst his peers. He would be a welcome addition to the ranks of PETTY OFFICER FIRST CLASS!!!

Attended Enlisted Professional Development Seminar; developed superior supervisory writing skills. Ready for promotion to PO1 now!

BM1 Smith is a master of his trade; I depend on his knowledge and expertise on all systems; Must Promote!

Chief Gonzalez is an astute Sailor. He has met all challenges at all levels and is ready to excel in any billet assigned. A clear choice for Senior Chief, Promote NOW!

Chief Jones' exceptional leadership, guidance, and dedication made it possible for VFC-13 to safely complete all assigned operational taskings during his watch while exceeding goals set by the Chief of Naval Operations for retention and personnel readiness.

Chief Smith is truly my "go to" Chief. Strongly recommend him for advancement to Senior Chief!

Chief Petty Officer Jones enjoys my complete trust and confidence. Promote to Senior Chief!

Chief Smith's SUSTAINED SUPERIOR PERFORMANCE is highly commendable. He has UNLIMITED POTENTIAL and is AN ABSOLUTE MUST SELECT FOR SENIOR CHIEF. PROMOTE HIM NOW!

Confident and dependable, he is quickly becoming an integral member of the Department. Promote.

Consistently committed to excellence. Petty Officer Jones is an intelligent, highly motivated leader. Extremely dedicated, hard working team player. Thrives in the dynamic environment of carrier aviation and has succeeded in the most demanding billet as workcenter supervisor. Possesses

all the characteristics of a strong leader. STRONGLY
ENDORSED FOR ADVANCEMENT TO CHIEF PETTY
OFFICER.

Consistently strives for improvement, working diligently
towards career progression; recommend immediate
ADVANCEMENT

Demonstrates the confidence needed to face the Navy's
toughest challenges. Promote to his potential.

Dependable SCPO; my ability to trust him with command on
a daily basis has provided new opportunities for growth.

Dependable, motivated, and trustworthy; a SCPO with the
courage to manage without visible support.

Determined and industrious professional. Petty Officer
Smith continually seeks personal growth and development.
Excels wherever assigned. Possesses the qualities of a
natural, exceptional leader. Constantly demonstrated strong
management and technical knowledge and abilities that
illustrate his limitless capacity. Has my strongest
endorsement for advancement to Chief Petty Officer.

Displays exceptional leadership qualities and the ability to
get the job done; recommend promotion/retention

Dynamic and distinguished CPO; leads by example; sets
high, yet attainable standards. Promote immediately.

DYNAMIC LEADER and MENTOR: His success in filling
critical manning deficiencies enabled DISA-EUR to maintain
the highest state of personnel readiness.

Enterprising and enthusiastic Yeoman. Petty Officer Smith manages each task to completion and total quality results are assured. Impressive military bearing and unwavering loyalty and appearance. Excellent communication skills. MOST STRONGLY RECOMMENDED FOR ADVANCEMENT TO CHIEF PETTY OFFICER.

Excelled as Construction Foreman, a post normally held by a seasoned SCPO; assumed new duties with an uncommon zeal. Assign to next rate now.

Exceptional Patient Administrator committed to successful completion of all assigned tasks. Must promote with peers!

Exceptional performer! Further challenge with most difficult tasks. Promote ahead of peers!

Extremely qualified, conscientious, and goal-oriented leader, whose personal initiative and drive consistently produce outstanding results. Totally dedicated to command mission accomplishment. Fully supports command equal opportunity program. Proficient writing and speaking ability. Maintains a perpetually well groomed personal appearance. Exemplary character, integrity, and loyalty. Favored over peers for promotion to Chief Petty Officer.

FC1 Smith was a major factor in the Bainbridge's most successful super trial in the history of the Arleigh Burke program, as the Combat Systems Team scored a perfect 1.0 on the INSURV Detect to Engage AAW Ops Demo.

FEARLESS AND DEDICATED, Petty Officer Jones takes on challenges most others avoid. He exhibits natural leadership and management abilities and leads subordinates with a mutual loyalty that is previously unknown. With unwavering allegiance to the chain of command, his achievements are marked by integrity and maturity. Approved for advancement to Chief Petty Officer.

First rate professional! Shows ability and initiative to assume greater responsibility--promote now

Flexible and versatile leader with unbounded potential, ready to assume SCPO responsibilities!

FN1 Gonzalez is a master of his trade; I rely daily on his knowledge and expertise on the system configuration; promote to capitalize on his skills

Forceful and dynamic leader. Aggressively completes tasks with confidence and professionalism. Exhibits a mature and professional attitude in all management practices. His efforts have justified my urgent insistence that he gain the next available slot for Chief.

Future Chief - SELECT AT EARLIEST POSSIBLE OPPORTUNITY!

GIFTED, INSPIRATIONAL MANAGER. Petty Officer Smith consistently demonstrates versatility, innovation, and perseverance in a high ops tempo environment and has forged an exemplary relationship of trust and concern with team members. Already serving in that capacity, make it official!

GIFTED, INSPIRING LEADER. Petty Officer Jones has taken charge and produced immediate results. A self-starter who motivates and inspires subordinates to perform to the absolute best of their ability. Demands and receives top quality performance. Has earned my strongest possible recommendation for immediate advancement. PROMOTE TO CHIEF PETTY OFFICER NOW!!

Goal orientated top achiever who gets results. Constantly exceeds all performance standards. His outstanding technical knowledge and leadership skills contribute to his boundless potential. He has my strongest possible personal recommendation for advancement to Chief Petty Officer and commissioning through the LDO Program.

Good performer; accomplished complex tasks with minimal supervision; works well with peers; must promote!

Great technician; knowledgeable on all workcenter communications systems; Early Promote

Hard charging Sailor whose willingness to accept responsibility for unpopular but necessary programs set him apart from his peers. Keep this comrade at the top; Promote!

Has shown a rare consistency in work ethic, continuing to be reliable and steady under all conditions

He is Master Chief material and is ready now to assume greater responsibilities. He possesses untapped potential to excel and should be placed in only the most demanding billets.

He is well-rounded in every performance category and has been thoroughly vetted for Senior Chief Petty Officer. He exemplifies excellence and is a perfect candidate for Senior Enlisted Advisor. PROMOTE TO SENIOR CHIEF NOW!

Highly recommended for assignment to positions requiring mature and dependable leadership. Recommended for advancement to Chief Petty Officer.

His diligent efforts and resourcefulness inspired all around him and contributed directly to the ability of his team to assume his duties in his absence.

His record of superior performance epitomizes professionalism. His attention to detail, motivation, and effective communication skills have established him as the top Petty Officer at this command.

His technical expertise and knowledge of CESE was invaluable in ensuring maximum equipment readiness and greatly enhanced the battalion's ability to complete mission taskings.

HMC Smith is a superstar, clearly excelling in a demanding assignment. He is an excellent candidate for Senior Chief. PROMOTE TO SENIOR CHIEF NOW AND KEEP HIM MOVING!

I have 100% confidence in her ability to ascend and perform as a First Class Storekeeper.

Immeasurable benefit to department and command. Petty Officer Jones has excelled as Armory Chief; his department has consistently passed all inspections and continues to set standards for the battalion.

Impeccable military bearing, loyalty, and appearance. Excellent communication skills. Most strongly recommended for advancement to Chief Petty Officer.

Intelligent and competent leader. Petty Officer Smith's keen ability to influence, guide, and train junior personnel has been the foundation of the Line Division's success. Advance to Chief Petty Officer.

IT1 Smith is a quality Petty Officer; displayed knowledge, drive, and initiative in completing all tasks-->promote now!

IT2 Jones is a dynamic leader and has my STRONGEST recommendation for advancement to Chief!

ITC1 Smith has shown tremendous growth, has overcome all obstacles, and is ready for a more challenging billet. A clear choice for Chief Petty Officer, Promote NOW!

Maintained 100% operational capability and accountability of $30 million worth of equipment under difficult circumstances. Demonstrates readiness for increased challenges. Promote!

Maintained a $30 million property account with a 98% accuracy, the best accountability of ten sections. Prime candidate for increased responsibilities

Maintains an immaculate military appearance and is steadfastly loyal. Fiercely supports the Navy's Equal Opportunity Program. MOST STRONGLY RECOMMENDED FOR ADVANCEMENT.

Managed 120 personnel in 5 demanding work centers: clearly demonstrates the potential for increased management responsibility

Mature and confident Seaman with extraordinary knowledge and experience. Immediately promote to E-7!

MC1 Smith is an outstanding Mass Communications Specialist and leading member of my staff who I nominate for our most challenging and demanding jobs. PROMOTE TO CPO and continue to detail to the Navy's most critical PA billets. He is a true superstar.

Motivated and dependable, a superior SCPO mature enough to make and enforce unpopular decisions when necessary.

My #1 of 15 Chief Petty Officers by a wide margin!

My #1 Petty Officer; selected as Health Services Manager of the Year 2009. Promote ahead of peers!

My go-to manager for replenishing planning; an outstanding Chief Petty Officer with exceptional experience and utterly reliable guidance; promote to SCPO now!

My number one Mobility line troop. Can always be counted on to ensure compliance with requirements

My number one Petty Officer; proven, exemplary track record confirms he is ready for immediate promotion!

None better at what they do! Should already be a Chief Petty Officer. PROMOTE IMMEDIATELY!

One of my best. A highly skilled and consistent stand out performer recognized by INSURV. Promote now!

OUTSTANDING Petty Officer who is scorching the competition. A true leader who developed a meaningful Chief's Mess that focuses on the command's success. PROMOTE TO CHIEF NOW!

Outstanding PO2! Achievements were key to ship winning 2008 COMNAVSURFLANT Blakely Cup--#1 of 12 ships

Petty Officer Jones' performance, both militarily and professionally, is nothing short of outstanding. A cheerful and hard-working individual, he enthusiastically participates in all Department duties. Dignified appearance, reflecting obvious pride in self and service. He is highly recommended for advancement to First Class Petty Officer.

Petty Officer Smith is a gem with multi-faceted talents and unlimited potential. He is strongly recommended for advancement and retention.

Petty Officer Smith is an asset to the Combined Bachelors Quarters and the United States Navy. His peerless performance has contributed significantly to the high level of success achieved by this command. He has our strongest backing for advancement to First Class Petty Officer.

PERFECT COMBINATION OF TECHNICAL EXCELLENCE AND DECKPLATE LEADERSHIP. PROMOTE TO CHIEF PETTY OFFICER NOW!

Personally committed to total quality and performance. Steadfastly loyal to this command and the Navy. Exceptionally skilled in planning and organizing. Will excel in any demanding position. Managerial and leadership abilities are second to none. Has my strongest personal endorsement for immediate selection to Chief Petty Officer and all programs leading to a commission.

Petty Officer Gonzalez is a dynamic and exceptionally resourceful leader that consistently produces superior results on all tasks while instilling and reinforcing professional core competencies in his personnel.

Petty Officer Jones is already performing at the Chief Petty Officer level. He should be assigned to our most critical and responsible leadership positions. Select for CPO NOW!

Petty Officer Jones' exemplary conduct and dedication to duty have earned the respect of everyone in his watch section as well as Senior Petty Officers.

Petty Officer Smith is a dedicated, cheerful, and hard-working individual who performs all duties in a thoughtful and enthusiastic manner. Always contributes full measure to any task and his willingness to accept added responsibility increases his potential for positions of more responsibility.

Petty Officer Jones' performance, both on duty and off , is nothing short of remarkable. Merits my sincere recommendation for promotion!

Petty Officer Smith is an ambitious Sailor with a desire for challenge. A buoyant leader who continuously motivates others to follow, his positive effect on the Department is readily apparent. Strongly recommended for advancement.

Petty Officer Smith is a natural leader. Possesses a unique blend of common sense and technical savvy. Staunchly loyal to this command and the Navy. Will excel in any demanding position. Impeccable military bearing and personal appearance. Approved for immediate selection to Chief Petty Officer.

Petty Officer Smith is a proven achiever of the highest caliber. Already performing at the Chief Petty Officer level, his impeccable appearance and military bearing are his trademarks. Conduct and devotion to duty are beyond reproach. He has earned his selection for promotion.

Petty Officer Jones is a TOP ACHIEVER who is able to plan, coordinate, and supervise the most complex activities. A proven leader with the technical knowledge of a recent A-school graduate and the managerial ability of a seasoned Chief, he is at the top of his game.

Petty Officer Smith is a top notch administrator with superb oral and written communication skills and a talent for staff work. She has exceptional potential for further professional growth and development. Strongly recommended for advancement to Chief Petty Officer.

Petty Officer Smith's knowledge of USNAVEUR and USNAVCENT operating procedures has been invaluable in training new personnel and ensuring the efficient handling of joint operational requirements.

Petty Officer Smith's take charge attitude and "can do" spirit paired with his natural ability made him my first choice for Watch Section Supervisor. He has unlimited potential for future leadership positions with increased authority and responsibility. Highly recommended for advancement.

Petty Officer Jones constantly delivered outstanding results and consistently went above and beyond the call of duty, always willing to volunteer for additional duties and responsibilities far beyond what was expected of someone in his position. YN2 Jones' remarkable performance and support over the last several months and throughout several multi-unit events has been an invaluable service to both the department and the United States Navy.

Petty Officer Smith is a Petty Officer with a high level of initiative and dedication. He has consistently demonstrated and uncommon level of performance throughout his tour at the Command. He is very deserving of this overall 5.0 evaluation and is recommended for advancement.

Phenomenal Sailor; surpassed every expectation in training and duty performance; ready for promotion now!

PN1 Smith is an absolutely superior Petty Officer; challenge with greater responsibility; must promote immediately!

PN1 Jones is ready for immediate promotion to PNC. He has the mental maturity and administrative knowledge to be an outstanding Limited Duty Officer and is strongly recommended for a commissioning program.

Petty Officer Gonzalez is excelling in a challenging position and already operating at the next level. Promote to Chief now!

Petty Officer Smith is as good as they get! Enjoys my strongest possible recommendation for immediate selection to Chief

PO1 Smith is a dedicated member of our team. His allegiance to the mission inspires his peers and make this Petty Officer an invaluable asset. Promote.

PO1 Jones is a superior Petty Officer and Communicator; NCTAMSLANT Sailor of the Quarter. Definitely promote now!

PO1 Smith is a dedicated team player who possesses outstanding leadership and management skills that are the driving force behind the detachment's success. SELECT FOR CHIEF NOW!!

Poised for achievement. Aggressively pursued and completed all requirements for the United Services Military Apprenticeship Program and is clearly capable of more advanced responsibilities.

Promotes high morale and encourages maximum participation and attainment of command goals. Ready to assume higher responsibilities and more demanding tasks.

Recent Air Force Leadership School graduate; poised to accept more challenging duties. Ready to promote.

Recipient of COMSUBLANT Superior Performer Award for December 09; promote ahead of peers!

Revised training qualification program; reduced required training for site qualification, reducing qualification time by 50% and increased productivity! Recommend for management post.

Rock solid in every category of performance! He has my strongest recommendation for retention and advancement. He is an excellent and deserving candidate for the Chief Petty Officer cadre. AN ABSOLUTE MUST PROMOTE TO CPO!

SA Smith is a very talented, well trained electronics and systems technician who inspires her peers to excellence.

Seaman Jones displays a keen aptitude for increased responsibility. Contributes full measure to any task and enthusiastically accepts added responsibility. He has my strongest possible recommendation for advancement to Petty Officer Second Class.

Senior Chief Petty Officer Smith enjoys my complete trust and confidence. Promote to Master Chief.

Senior Chief Petty Officer Smith has excelled at and outgrown his responsibilities as SCPO. Promote to Master Chief now!

Senior Chief Petty Officer Smith has repeatedly earned my complete trust and confidence. Promote to Master Chief!

Senior Chief Smith exemplifies our core values and brings out the best in those around him. He possesses all the qualities of an outstanding Command Senior Chief. He has my strongest personal recommendation for Master Chief Petty Officer.

Senior Chief Smith has my strongest recommendation for selection as Chief of the Boat and immediate advancement to Master Chief Petty Officer

Senior Chief Smith is excelling in a tough position and already operating at the next level. PROMOTE TO MASTER CHIEF NOW!

Senior Chief Smith is a driven SCPO with outstanding results. Continue to entrust with increasing responsibility. Promote now!

SN Jones is a hard working, versatile Sailor. Quickly work center qualified. Challenge with more responsibilities.

SN Smith is a dynamic Sailor and multi-talented mechanic. He readily accepts increased responsibilities. Promote Now!

SN Jones possesses a strong record of credibility, loyalty, and dedication. A true team player. Promote now!

Solid performer; displays exceptional leadership qualities /abilities. Recommend promotion soonest

Star performer! Received only billet available from the Command for promotion to ET1

Superior leader and professional; sets high standards for his peers and subordinates to emulate; ready for promotion and greater responsibility

Supervises two Sailors; both are ahead of their peers in work center qualification . A born leader, promote at first opportunity.

The ability to inspire the enlisted to do their best despite all obstacles set this leader apart. Unmatched foresight and accomplishment, a true standout at Fleet HQ. He has my strongest recommendation for immediate advancement to Master Chief Petty Officer.

The most conscientious, loyal, and dedicated Petty Officer I've served with in 20 years-- Promote to Chief Now!

This is the one to become our next MCPON!

Top 15% of my Chief Petty Officers; superior technical expertise paired with unmatched motivation. Promote to Senior Chief!

Top-notch leader. Petty Officer Smith is without a doubt one of the most impressive First Class Petty Officers that I have had the pleasure to work with. His leadership, managerial, and technical abilities are second to none.

Awards

In the Navy, there are three broad categories of awards: unit awards, service awards, and personal awards. Unit awards are earned by the unit and may be worn by its members. Examples are the Presidential Unit Citation and the Navy Unit Commendation. They aren't worth any points but they look good on your rack.

Service awards are earned by participation in deployments and campaigns. Examples of service awards are the Armed Forces Expeditionary Medal and the Overseas Service Ribbon.

This section is about the last category of awards, personal awards. Examples of personal awards are the Navy and Marine Corps Achievement Medal and the Navy and Marine Corps Commendation Medal. Personal awards are worth points toward promotion and are a key factor in a Sailor's chances for promotion. They are commonly presented to recognize exemplary service. It has become so common, in fact, that every supervisor must ensure their troops receive the awards they've earned just so they can remain competitive for promotion. If you haven't submitted someone for a medal before it might seem somewhat challenging but it's not really that hard. Most award packages only require a few minutes of preparation and follow a prescribed format which is documented in SECNAVINST 1650.1H, Navy and Marine Corps Awards Manual. The benefits far outweigh the little effort required.

For instructions on the most commonly awarded medals, the Navy and Marine Corps Achievement Medal and the Navy and Marine Corps Commendation Medal, see the next sections.

Navy Achievement Medal

Achievement medals are worth 2 points toward promotion. Prepare recommendations for personal decorations on the Personal Award Recommendation Form (Navy: OPNAV 1650/3; Marine Corps: NAVMC 11533 (EF)). Marine Corps units use the electronic awards submission system to prepare awards.

Since each recommendation for award is evaluated on the merits of the justification, normally a Summary of Action (block 25) is required but, in the case of Navy Command awarded Navy and Marine Corps Achievement Medals, a Summary of Action is not required. The Marine Corps requires the achievement award to have a short, bullet-format summary. When writing justifications and citations, generalities and the excessive use of superlatives (grand, illustrious, and superfluous) should be avoided. A concrete description of what the person actually accomplished is preferred.

A proposed citation, which is a condensed version of the summary of action, must accompany the recommendation. So, in summary, all you need to prepare for an Achievement medal is the OPNAV 1650, Personal Award Recommendation and a separate citation typed on plain bond paper. Specific instructions for filling out the 1650 follow.

OPNAV 1650/3 Instructions

FROM: Include command long and short titles of the originator listed in block 22 with complete address and a point of contact (POC) and DSN phone number.

TO: Proper awarding authority (see SECNAVINST 1650.1G, Navy and Marine Corps Awards Manual, Appendix B, chapter 1) with complete address and UIC.

1. SOCIAL SECURITY NUMBER: Social Security Number of the person who is being recommended for an award.

2. DESIG/NEC/MOS:
a. DESIG is for officer designator, such as 1110, 1705, etc.
b. NEC is Navy Enlisted Classification Code. The primary NEC should be used. If the person has no code, enter 0000 (four zeros).
c. MOS: This is the USMC Military Occupational Specialty.

3. NAME. Type the person's last name first (ALL CAPITAL LETTERS), followed by a comma (,), then type first name, middle initial and any suffixes, i.e., Jr., Sr., II, III etc.

4. COMPONENT: As shown on the form, either USN, USNR, USNR (TAR), USNR-R, USMC, or USMCR.

5. GRADE/RATE: For the person being recommended use the authorized abbreviation, i.e., CAPT, CDR, LCDR, LT, LTJG, ENS, CWO4, YNCM, YNC, or DPSA. (Don't use O2, E7, E5 etc.)

6. WARFARE DESIGNATOR: Use primary warfare designator, e.g., SW, AW, etc. If multiple, only the first one will be recognized.

7. UIC/RUIC: This is the Unit Identification Code (UIC) to which the person was/is assigned during the period of recommended award.

8. RECOMMENDED AWARD: NAVY AND MARINE CORPS ACHIEVEMENT MEDAL - NA.

9. SPECIFIC ACHIEVEMENT. Mark Yes if award is for specific achievement. If award is a tour award, mark No.

10. SELF-EXPLANATORY. The majority of peacetime awards will be "meritorious".

11. NUMBER OF AWARD OF THIS MEDAL: If the person being recommended has never received an Achievement Medal before, type in "FIRST". If this will be the "second" or "third" award, then indicate, "SECOND", "THIRD", etc.

12. ACTION DATE/MERITORIOUS PERIOD: This block requests the complete start/stop dates of period covered for recommended award.

13. GEOGRAPHIC AREA OF ACTION/SERVICE: e.g. CONUS, WESTPAC, MED, EUROPE, CARIBBEAN, etc.

14. EXP. OF ACTIVE DUTY: For officers, this is usually "INDEFINITE," unless the officer is retiring or otherwise leaving the Naval Service, in which case, type in retirement date or last day of active duty. For enlisted personnel, type in EAOS (expiration of active obligated service).

15. EST. DETACHMENT DATE: The date the person is scheduled to depart the command, whether departing for PCS or terminal leave. Include exact date if known. Mark appropriate box - retirement etc. If ceremony is scheduled on a different date, type it in parenthesis, i.e., (ceremony 15 May 2005).

16. NEW DUTY STATION: Type in the SNDL-authorized short title of the new duty station and full mailing address, including ZIP code. If the individual is retiring or leaving the service, type in full HOME address, including ZIP code.

17. UNIT AT TIME OF ACTION/SERVICE: The unit to which the individual being recommended was assigned during the period covered by the proposed award.

18. DUTY ASSIGNMENT: Type in a brief general description of the person's title during the period the award is recommended for, e.g., Commanding Officer, OPS Officer, Flight Instructor, Flag Writer, Command Master Chief, Clerk, etc.

19. PREVIOUS PERSONAL DECORATIONS AND PERIOD RECOGNIZED: Examples of personal decorations are the Navy and Marine Corps Achievement Medal and the Meritorious Service Medal. Do not list Service awards (such as the Navy Good Conduct Medal) or Unit awards (such as the Navy Unit Commendation). Ensure the period covered for each personal award is included. Attach a copy of any award(s) which overlap the period of the recommended award.

20. PERSONAL AWARDS RECOMMENDED - NOT YET APPROVED: Normally, "NONE."

21. OTHER PERSONNEL BEING RECOMMENDED FOR SAME ACTION: Normally, "NONE." For life-saving actions when a group is recommended for the same action, list other personnel. Forward awards together.

22. NAME, GRADE, TITLE OF ORIGINATOR: For example, John P. Jones, RADM, Director of Naval Intelligence. The originator must sign and date the form as well as check one of the two boxes above the signature block.

23. FORWARDING ENDORSEMENTS: As required by the chain of command.

24. To be completed by the Awarding Authority. This must be completed by the command making final disposition. Use the two-letter code for the approved award and check the appropriate boxes. All awarding authorities must sign and date the approval. (Signature should correspond to the "To: (Awarding Authority) Block" above.

25. SUMMARY OF ACTION: The summary of action is not required for Command-approved Navy and Marine Corps Achievement Medals (Navy only). For Marine Corps, all awards require a summary of action in bullet statement format. Specific information/accomplishments are essential to the narrative summary. Ensure that the dates in Block 11 match the dates listed in this block, as well as the proposed citation. A one-page summary of action will suffice in most cases.

Notes:

FOR NONCOMBAT AWARDS

- Brevity is encouraged.

- Outline or bullet format limited to one page is sufficient in the majority of cases.

- Emphasis should be on specific accomplishments of individual that set that person apart from his/her peers.

COMBAT AWARDS

- Must be fully justified.

- Eyewitness statement (at least two if practicable).

FOR LIFE SAVING AWARDS

- If practicable, include statements of at least two eyewitnesses. Such statements should furnish accounts of the incident, including opinions as to whether the person for whom the award is sought imperiled his/her life. Police reports and newspaper accounts can also be submitted.

- The precise locality of the rescue or attempted rescue, or heroic action.

- The date, time of day, nature of weather, including force of the wind, condition and temperature of the water if applicable, and amount and source of light if at night.

- The names of all persons rendering assistance and the nature of the assistance.

- A freehand sketch of the scene, including distances, location of assistance, and heights of piers or vessels from which rescue efforts were started, as applicable.

- A statement as to the swimming qualifications of the rescuer if applicable. (See art. 6610120, MILPERS Manual for Navy personnel; and NAVMC 2779 for Marine Corps personnel.)

- An account of the cooperation or lack thereof on the part of the person being rescued.

- A rescue from burning should be described in great detail, including the aid received by the rescuer, the extent of the burns, and a description of the outer clothing of the rescuer.

- It is emphasized that recommendations should include the above, but should not necessarily be limited to that information.

Citation Instructions

The proposed citation, which is a summary of the action being recognized, must accompany the recommendation for award. The proposed citation should be prepared in double space, all upper case type, Courier New 10 pitch font, and without acronyms. It must be factual and may not include classified information. Non-combat citations are limited to 7 ½ lines.

A citation consists of three parts:

1. Opening Sentence. The citation begins with a standard phrase (dictated by regulation) describing the degree of meritorious or heroic service as specified for each award, duty assignment of the individual, inclusive dates of service on which the recommendation is based, and if desired, a description of operations of the unit to which the individual is attached. The following opening phrase is used for the Navy Achievement Medal:

"For professional achievement in the superior performance of his/her duties while serving as..."

2. Statement of Achievement or Service. The second part of the citation identifies the recipient by name, describes specific duty assignments, his/her accomplishments and the outstanding personal attributes displayed. The description of the individual's achievements must show clearly that they were sufficient to justify the award recommended. The value of results of achievements may also be included. If duty was performed in actual combat, the citation should so state.

3. Commendatory Remarks. The third part of the citation states that the outstanding attributes, mentioned or implied in the second part, "reflected great credit upon him/her and were in keeping with the highest traditions of the United States Naval Service." (or "of the Marine Corps and the United States Naval Service." for Marines)

There are two options for the format of the last sentence. Use whichever sounds best:

OPTION 1. Beginning with *the individual's name*:

"Petty Officer Doe's managerial ability, personal initiative, and unswerving devotion to duty reflected great credit upon him and were in keeping with the highest traditions of the United States Naval Service."

OR

OPTION 2. Beginning with *the three attributes*:

"By his managerial ability, personal initiative, and unswerving devotion to duty, Petty Officer Doe reflected great credit upon himself and upheld the highest traditions of the United States Naval Service."

Note: The attributes listed in the last sentence of the example citation (*MANAGERIAL ABILITY, PERSONAL INITIATIVE, AND UNSWERVING DEVOTION TO DUTY*) are not mandatory. They are merely listed as an example. Attributes appropriate for the individual and the circumstances of the award should be used. Examples of commonly used attributes are:

NOTEWORTHY ACCOMPLISHMENTS, PERSEVERANCE AND DEVOTION TO DUTY

UNSWERVING DETERMINATION, WISE JUDGMENT, AND COMPLETE DEDICATION TO DUTY

INITIATIVE, PERSEVERANCE, AND TOTAL DEDICATION TO DUTY REFLECT

VAST TECHNICAL AND PROFESSIONAL KNOWLEDGE COUPLED WITH HER EXCEPTIONAL LEADERSHIP ABILITIES

DILIGENT PREPARATION, SKILLFUL INSTRUCTION, AND RELENTLESS EFFORTS

TECHNICAL SKILLS, PERSONAL INITIATIVE AND LOYAL DEVOTION TO DUTY

EXCEPTIONAL ABILITY, PERSONAL INITIATIVE AND TOTAL DEDICATION TO DUTY

EXCEPTIONAL LEADERSHIP, INITIATIVE, AND LOYAL DEDICATION TO DUTY

General guidelines.

The rank, name, and service are all capital letters and centered. Due to the length of enlisted rates, three lines are used; warfare designation is not required, but the primary designation is used when space is available. Additional designations are never appropriate.

Officers use two lines with rank and name combined; a third line, for staff corps designation is optional.

For Marine Corps personnel, two lines shall be used for the individual's grade, name, and service.

In accordance with NAVADMIN 121/05, the service for all Navy personnel (whether active or reserve component) shall be "UNITED STATES NAVY."

Use all capital letters for the Navy and Marine Corps Commendation or Achievement Medals. All other citations require upper and lower case.

There can be many varieties of style for the same award; awarding authorities may dictate specific guidance for awards under their authority as long as they meet the basic requirements cited above.

DEPARTMENT OF THE NAVY

THIS IS TO CERTIFY THAT
THE SECRETARY OF THE NAVY HAS AWARDED THE

NAVY AND MARINE CORPS ACHIEVEMENT MEDAL

(GOLD STAR / COMBAT DISTINGUISHING DEVICE)

TO

SENIOR CHIEF AVIATION MACHINIST'S MATE JANE W. DOE, UNITED STATES NAVY

PROFESSIONAL ACHIEVEMENT AS MAINTENANCE CONTROL CHIEF PETTY OFFICER FOR HELICOPTER ANTISUBMARINE SQUADRON LIGHT FORTY TWO FROM MARCH 1989 TO AUGUST 1993. SENIOR CHIEF PETTY OFFICER DOE CONTRIBUTED SIGNIFICANTLY TO THE SUCCESSFUL INTRODUCTION OF LAMPS MK III TO THE FLEET BY DEVELOPING A RESPONSIVE MAINTENANCE CONTROL TEAM TO SUPPORT 15 DETACHMENTS DEPLOYED WORLDWIDE. SHE DISPLAYED EXCEPTIONAL TECHNICAL EXPERTISE IN ASSISTING DETACHMENTS DURING BOTH THE CHALLENGER AND LIBYAN OPERATIONS. HER MANAGERIAL ABILITY, PERSONAL INITIATIVE, AND UNSWERVING DEVOTION TO DUTY REFLECTED CREDIT UPON HER AND WERE IN KEEPING WITH THE HIGHEST TRADITIONS OF THE UNITED STATES NAVAL SERVICE.

DEPARTMENT OF THE NAVY

THIS IS TO CERTIFY THAT
THE SECRETARY OF THE NAVY HAS AWARDED THE

NAVY AND MARINE CORPS ACHIEVEMENT MEDAL

(SILVER STAR IN LIEU OF THE SIXTH AWARD)

TO

CHIEF YEOMAN (SURFACE WARFARE) JOHN L. DOE, UNITED STATES NAVY

FOR

PROFESSIONAL ACHIEVEMENT AS RECORDER FOR THE PHYSICAL EVALUATION BOARD, SECRETARY OF THE NAVY COUNCIL OF REVIEW BOARDS FROM MAY 2005 TO AUGUST 2007. CHIEF PETTY OFFICER DOE'S INSPIRING LEADERSHIP AND PERSONAL INITIATIVE WERE INSTRUMENTAL IN THE EFFICIENT AND TIMELY PROCESSING OF MORE THAN 50,000 NAVY AND MARINE CORPS ACTIVE DUTY AND RESERVE DISABILITY CASES, AND COMBAT RELATED SPECIAL COMPENSATION (CRSC) CASES. HE CONTINUALLY EDUCATED PERSONNEL ON THE INTRICACIES OF THE CRSC SYSTEM. CHIEF PETTY OFFICER DOE'S EXCEPTIONAL PROFESSIONALISM, UNRELENTING PERSEVERANCE, AND LOYAL DEVOTION TO DUTY REFLECTED CREDIT UPON HIM AND WERE IN KEEPING WITH THE HIGHEST TRADITIONS OF THE UNITED STATES NAVAL SERVICE.

Notes:

If applicable, the Gold Star or Combat "V" should be added above the 'To' line.

Citations for the Navy and Marine Corps Achievement Medals shall be prepared in all upper case letters in Courier New, size 10, and are limited to 7 1/2 typewritten lines with margins of one inch.

For combat awards, replace the words 'meritorious service' with 'heroic achievement'.

Navy Commendation Medal

Commendation medals are worth 3 points and are counted toward promotion. Recommendations for personal decorations are submitted using the Personal Award Recommendation Form: OPNAV 1650/3 for the Navy; Marine Corps use NAVMC 11533 (EF). Marine Corps units use the electronic awards submission system to prepare awards.

Normally a Summary of Action (block 25) must be completed to justify an award but, in the case of the Navy Command-awarded Navy and Marine Corps Commendation Medal for Navy personnel, a Summary of Action is not required. The Marine Corps requires the award to have a short, bullet-format summary.

When writing justifications for awards and citations, generalities and the excessive use of unnecessary adjectives (superb, outstanding, etc) should be avoided. A concrete description of what the person actually achieved is preferred.

A citation, which is a condensed version of the summary of action, must accompany the recommendation for award.

In summary, the only documentation required to submit a Commendation Medal package is the OPNAV 1650/3, Personal Award Recommendation, and a separate citation typed on plain bond paper. Specific instructions for filling out the 1650 follow.

OPNAV 1650/3 Instructions

FROM: Include command long and short titles of the originator listed in block 22 with complete address and a point of contact (POC) and DSN phone number.

TO: Proper awarding authority (see SECNAVINST 1650.1G, Navy and Marine Corps Awards Manual, Appendix B, chapter 1) with complete address and UIC.

1. SOCIAL SECURITY NUMBER: Social security number of the person who is being recommended for an award.

2. DESIG/NEC/MOS:
a. DESIG is for officer designator, such as 1110, 1705, etc.
b. NEC is Navy Enlisted Classification Code. The primary NEC should be used. If the person has no code, enter 0000 (four zeros).
c. MOS: This is the USMC Military Occupational Specialty.

3. NAME. Type the person's last name first (ALL CAPITAL LETTERS), followed by a comma (,), then type first name, middle initial and any suffixes, i.e., Jr., Sr., II, III etc.

4. COMPONENT: As shown on the form, either USN, USNR, USNR (TAR), USNR-R, USMC, or USMCR.

5. GRADE/RATE: For the person being recommended use the authorized abbreviation, i.e., CAPT, CDR, LCDR, LT, LTJG, ENS, CWO4, YNCM, YNC, or DPSA. (Don't use O2, E7, E5 etc.)

6. WARFARE DESIGNATOR: Use primary warfare designator, e.g., SW, AW, etc. If multiple, only the first one will be recognized.

7. UIC/RUIC: This is the Unit Identification Code (UIC) to which the person was/is assigned during the period of recommended award.

8. RECOMMENDED AWARD: NAVY AND MARINE CORPS COMMENDATION MEDAL – NC (Use appropriate 2 letter code from back of form.)

9. SPECIFIC ACHIEVEMENT. Mark Yes if award is for specific achievement. If award is a tour award, mark No.

10. SELF-EXPLANATORY. The majority of peacetime awards will be "meritorious".

11. NUMBER OF AWARD OF THIS MEDAL: If the person being recommended has never received the recommended award, type in "FIRST". If this will be *"second" or "third", then indicate "SECOND", "THIRD", etc.*

12. ACTION DATE/MERITORIOUS PERIOD: This block requests the complete start/stop dates of period covered for recommended award.

13. GEOGRAPHIC AREA OF ACTION/SERVICE: e.g. CONUS, WESTPAC, MED, EUROPE, CARIBBEAN, etc.

14. EXP. OF ACTIVE DUTY: For officers, this is usually "INDEFINITE," unless the officer is retiring or otherwise leaving the Naval Service, in which case, type in retirement date or last day of active duty. For enlisted personnel, type in EAOS (expiration of active obligated service).

15. EST. DETACHMENT DATE: The date the person is scheduled to depart the command, whether departing for PCS or terminal leave. Include exact date if known. Mark appropriate box - retirement etc. If ceremony is scheduled on a different date, type it in parenthesis, i.e., (ceremony 15 Oct 2005).

16. NEW DUTY STATION: Type in the SNDL-authorized short title of the new duty station and full mailing address, including ZIP code. If the individual is retiring or leaving the service, type in full HOME address, including ZIP code.

17. UNIT AT TIME OF ACTION/SERVICE: The unit to which the individual being recommended was assigned during the period covered by the proposed award.

18. DUTY ASSIGNMENT: Type in a brief general description of the person's title during the period the award is recommended for, e.g., Commanding Officer, OPS Officer, Flight Instructor, Flag Writer, Command Master Chief, Clerk, etc.

19. PREVIOUS PERSONAL DECORATIONS AND PERIOD RECOGNIZED: A personal decoration is one that is listed in 1650.1G Chapter 2. Examples of personal decorations are the Navy and Marine Corps Achievement Medal and the Meritorious Service Medal. Do not list Service awards (such as the Navy Good Conduct Medal) or Unit awards (such as the Navy Unit Commendation). Ensure the period covered for each personal award is included. Attach a copy of any award(s) which overlap the period of the recommended award.

20. PERSONAL AWARDS RECOMMENDED - NOT YET APPROVED: Normally, "NONE." Usually used for combat awards.

21. OTHER PERSONNEL BEING RECOMMENDED FOR SAME ACTION: Normally, "NONE." For life-saving actions when a group is recommended for the same action, list other personnel. Forward awards together.

22. NAME, GRADE, TITLE OF ORIGINATOR: For example, John P. Jones, RADM, Director of Naval Intelligence. The originator must sign and date the form as well as check one of the two boxes above the signature block.

23. FORWARDING ENDORSEMENTS: As required by the chain of command.

24. To be completed by the Awarding Authority. This must be completed by the command making final disposition. Use the two-letter code for the approved award and check the appropriate boxes. All awarding authorities must sign and date the approval. (Signature should correspond to the "To: (Awarding Authority) Block" above.

25. SUMMARY OF ACTION: This must be submitted for every award recommendation EXCEPT Command-approved Navy and Marine Corps Commendation Medals (NC) for Navy only. For Marine Corps, all awards require a bullet summary. Specific information/accomplishments are essential to the narrative summary. Ensure that the dates in Block 11 match exactly with the dates in this block as well as the proposed citation. A one-page summary of action will suffice in most cases.

See the additional instructions under the Navy Achievement Medal section concerning the award of combat awards and life saving awards

IN ALL CASES AN UNCLASSIFIED PROPOSED CITATION WILL BE SUBMITTED

Citation Instructions

A proposed citation, condensed from the Summary of Action, must accompany the recommendation. Although a citation is laudatory and formalized, it must be factual and contain no classified information.

The proposed citation shall be prepared in double space, upper and lower case type, and without acronyms. Non-combat citations are limited to 7 ½ lines. A citation consists of three parts:

(1) Opening Sentence. The citation begins with a standard phrase describing the degree of meritorious or heroic service as specified for each award, duty assignment of the individual, inclusive dates of service on which the recommendation is based, and if desired, a description of operations of the unit to which the individual is attached. The following opening phrase is used for the Navy Commendation Medal:

"For meritorious service (or meritorious achievement)(or heroic service)(or heroic achievement) while serving as..."

(2) Statement of Heroic/Meritorious Achievement or Service. The second part of the citation identifies the recipient by name, describes specific duty assignments, his/her accomplishments and the outstanding personal attributes displayed. The description of the individual's achievements must show clearly that they were sufficient to justify the award recommended. Value of results of achievements may also be included. If duty was performed in actual combat, the citation should so state.

(3) Commendatory Remarks. The third part of the citation states that the outstanding attributes, mentioned or implied in the second part, "reflected great credit upon him/her and were in keeping with the highest traditions of the United States Naval Service." (or "of the Marine Corps and the United States Naval Service." for Marines)

Note: The attributes listed in the last sentence of the example citation shown (*noteworthy accomplishments, perseverance, and devotion to duty*) are not mandatory. They are merely listed as an example. Attributes appropriate for the individual being recommended should be used.

There are two options for the format of the last sentence. Use whichever sounds best:

(1) Beginning with the individual's name: "Petty Officer Doe's bold leadership, wise judgment, and complete dedication to duty reflected great credit upon him and were in keeping with the highest traditions of the United States Naval Service."

OR

(2) Beginning with the three attributes: 'By his bold leadership, wise judgment, and complete dedication to duty, Petty Officer Doe reflected great credit upon himself and upheld the highest traditions of the United States Naval Service."

DEPARTMENT OF THE NAVY

THIS IS TO CERTIFY THAT
THE SECRETARY OF THE NAVY HAS AWARDED THE

NAVY AND MARINE CORPS COMMENDATION MEDAL

(GOLD STAR / COMBAT DEVICE)
TO
HOSPITAL CORPSMAN FIRST CLASS JANE S. DOE, UNITED STATES NAVY

MERITORIOUS SERVICE AS TRANSPLANTATION TECHNICIAN AT NAVAL HOSPITAL, SAN DIEGO, CALIFORNIA FROM JANUARY 1993 TO MARCH 1997. PETTY OFFICER DOE DESIGNED A TRANSPORTATION NETWORK FOR THE COLLECTION OF HUMAN TISSUE AND ORGANS, TRAINED TRANSPLANT TECHNICIANS, AND DEVELOPED A MACHINE TO PRODUCE ALLOGRAFT MATERIAL OF A UNIFORM SIZE AND HIGH QUALITY. HER INNOVATIVE ACTIONS IN NUMEROUS AREAS CONTRIBUTED TO THE ENHANCEMENT OF MILITARY HEALTH CARE DELIVERY AND PATIENT CARE. BY HER NOTEWORTHY ACCOMPLISHMENTS, PERSEVERANCE, AND DEVOTION TO DUTY, PETTY OFFICER DOE REFLECTED CREDIT UPON HERSELF AND UPHELD THE HIGHEST TRADITIONS OF THE UNITED STATES NAVAL SERVICE.

Navy Writer

DEPARTMENT OF THE NAVY

THIS IS TO CERTIFY THAT
THE SECRETARY OF THE NAVY HAS AWARDED THE

NAVY AND MARINE CORPS COMMENDATION MEDAL

(GOLD STAR / COMBAT "V")
TO
HOSPITAL CORPSMAN THIRD CLASS JOHN D. DOE, UNITED STATES NAVY

FOR

HEROIC ACHIEVEMENT WHILE SERVING AS A CORPSMAN FOR 2D SQUAD, WEAPONS PLATOON, COMPANY B, 4TH BATTALION, MARWEST, 1ST MARINE DIVISION, I MARINE EXPEDITIONARY FORCE, U.S. MARINE CORPS FORCES, CENTRAL IN SUPPORT OF OPERATION IRAQI FREEDOM ON 14 FEBRUARY 2005. WHILE ON PATROL, PETTY OFFICER DOE LEARNED AN IRAQI CIVILIAN HAD BEEN SHOT AND LEFT IN A CAR RIGGED WITH AN IMPROVISED EXPLOSIVE DEVICE (IED). DISREGARDING HIS OWN SAFETY, HE RAN TO THE CAR AND EXTRACTED THE CIVILIAN. SUDDENLY, THE IED DETONATED, WOUNDING PETTY OFFICER DOE. UNDAUNTED, HE CONTINUED TO SAFETY, SAVING THE CIVILIAN'S LIFE. BY HIS UNSWERVING DETERMINATION, WISE JUDGMENT, AND COMPLETE DEDICATION TO DUTY, PETTY OFFICER DOE REFLECTED CREDIT UPON HIMSELF AND UPHELD THE HIGHEST TRADITIONS OF THE UNITED STATES NAVAL SERVICE.

Notes:

If applicable, a Gold Star or Combat "V" may be added above the 'To' line.

Citations for the Navy and Marine Corps Commendation and Navy and Marine Corps Achievement Medals shall be prepared in all upper case letters in Courier New, size 10, and are limited to 7 1/2 typewritten lines with margins of one inch.

For combat awards, replace 'meritorious service' with 'heroic achievement'.

Made in the USA
Las Vegas, NV
30 November 2021

35679906R00144